guide click

Florence
for teens

welcome books

ISBN 88-8430-001-0

Text and editing: Sepia - Studio Redazionale, Florence
Translation: Elisabetta Coletti
Graphic design and jacket cover: Grazia Ghidoni / Sepia
Illustrations: Fiorella e Morena Cauduro
Photographs: Archivio Scala, Archivio K & B, Dario Grimoldi, Nicolò Orsi Battaglini, Alberto Pietrini, Giuliano Valsecchi.
We would like to thank the Museo Salvatore Ferragamo for the pictures on page 74.
And a special thanks goes to Italia Mariotti and the Fatatrac publishing house for giving permission to reproduce some of Mario Mariotti's work.
Reproductions: Fotolito Toscana, Firenze

First edition: May 2000

Reprints
5 4 3 2 1 2000 2001 2002 2003 2004

Table of Contents

"Click Club"

Elettra She plays the saxophone and is a super organizer – always thinks a lot before making decisions. She's great at solving problems. Even rebuses, anagrams, crossword puzzles, and word problems are a snap for her.

Sebastiano (Seba) He loves basketball and is a great cook. He's also in love with Gemma (who does most of his homework.) School is not his strong point, but he makes up for it with his delicious Bavarian cream desserts. Really fast with computers and knows all the best gourmet Web sites.

Alice She's really pretty – and a bit of a flirt. She adores animals and likes to go bird-watching. A health nut, she's also got a thing for Daja – her pen pal from India.

Plato Andrea's sheep dog. Quite a photography fan in his own right, he never misses a Click Club meeting.

Mattia Absolutely gorgeous. All the girls have crushes on him, but he is totally clueless. A tad obsessed with retouching photos, he tweaks every picture he gets his hands on. He likes taking walks alone and is a champion paraglider.

Chiara A mechanic at heart, she's taken her moped apart five times. She even tries to play Miss Fix-It with computers. A ballerina, she has no idea Boris likes her.

eniamino (Ben)
e is a flake and loses track of
ımost everything. He's not too
syched about computers, but he has
use them. He has this weird hobby
f collecting eyeglasses and is
opelessly in love with Florence,
hom he met on a field trip to France.

Andrea He plays soccer and is an all-around nice guy. He is awesome at telling jokes and has a dog named Plato (Andrea's biggest fan). He's got the hots for the substitute science teacher.

ile Modifica Visualizza Vai Preferite ?

The foreign pen pals

ARATA Computer and photography fanatic from Sapporo, Japan. He fil[redacted] everyone in on all th[redacted] latest high-tech news[redacted]He sings like Ricky Martin, collects stamps, and is not in love with anyone.

PAMELA[redacted]swimmer from Australia, a little on the[redacted]chubby side. She's always on a diet, [redacted]ut usually blows it by splurging and scarfing everything in sight. Blonde, extroverted, super-social. She's never set foot outside Australia. She's got a crush on her swim coach Bill, but it's hopeless.

BRAD He lives in Seattle (where it rains all the time) on a houseboat. Compute[redacted] stud, but also into mod[redacted] art and architecture. He trades photo-retouching programs and upgrades with Mattia. He met a Brazilian girl, Heloisa, while surfing online; now they write each other letters back and forth.

DAJA Lives in Calcutta, where he helps his Dad desig[redacted]ovie posters. He's[redacted]nterested in the kin[redacted]f filmmaking Ken Loac[redacted] does – documentaries. Really cute, with velvety eyes.

MIKA He lives in Finland on a lake that's frozen solid eight months out of the year. The closest city to his home is 70 miles away. He uses his computer to study, and likes ice skating and ice fishing. His best friend Beth is a geology whiz from Pretoria, South Africa.

May Day, 1459

There's a big party tonight at the palace on Via Larga. An enormous banquet is being held up on the second floor. Many of the evening's guests came to see visiting Pope Pius II, but he didn't feel like socializing and stayed at his Santa Maria Novella apartments. He says he's tired, but everyone knows he really can't stand Florentines (like any self-respecting guy from Siena!). In particular, he despises the Medici family, whom he calls "new-money peddlers strutting around their new palace."
The buzz of voices, instruments, and songs coming from the party drifts into the sand-covered street – brightly lit up by 150 double lampposts. There are a lot of big shots at the party, like: Lord Cecco Ordelaffi of Forlí, Lord Astorre Manfredi of Faenza, and Lord Sigismondo Pandolfo Malatesta of Rimini. But the most important (and lusted after) of all is the Duke of Milan's son: young Galeazzo Maria Sforza. At last, the party starts to move outdoors. People crowd into the streets and around the main gate. Some people peek out the first-floor windows.
From a distance, a long procession inches up the road. At the front is a very young boy, a 10-year-old named Lorenzo. He's the grandson of Cosimo dei Medici and the son of Piero. He proudly advances atop a white horse, clutching his red, white, and green banner with a falcon in the middle. Twelve knights file behind him – all sons of the city's most important families. Each knight is accompanied by a shield and 25 valets dressed in his family's colors. The "Armeggeria" is about to begin, when the 12 knights compete in a variety of events. The most popular of these is the contest to strike a target by throwing a long spear. These lances are made especially for the Armeggeria: hollow, constructed of light wood, and made up of many colorful segments that shatter upon impact with the targets. It is a spectacular sight when the spears break apart and fly through the air – with the crowd cheering. But that's not all; there's still one surprise left. There's the celebration for the winner, when he's carted about on a carriage amid explosions and sparks from pinwheels and fireworks.

Brief history of the city

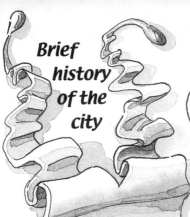

In the 10th-century BC, a village was founded at the confluence of two rivers: the Arno and the Mugnone. This was the beginning of what would become Florence. This village, possibly called Villa Arnina, was destroyed during a battle between two Roman commanders (Marius and Silla) in the 1st-century BC. In 59 BC, Silla defeated Marius and established a Roman colony where the old village had stood: "Florentia."

Florentia (which means abundance or wealth) becomes an important business hub for many centuries, and also the seat of the governor of Tuscany and Umbria. The city withstands numerous attacks by the Barbarians, until 570 AD when the Lombards conquer it. They go on to establish their own representative, a duke, as governor.

During the Carolingian period (late 8th-century) Florence expands and becomes even more beautiful. On three separate occasions, the city plays host to Charlemagne, who then makes Florence a county of his Holy Roman Empire. And so, Florentine Bishops become very powerful, bolstering their coffers with noble titles, land grants, and plum religious appointments.

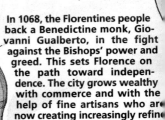

In 1068, the Florentines people back a Benedictine monk, Giovanni Gualberto, in the fight against the Bishops' power and greed. This sets Florence on the path toward independence. The city grows wealthy with commerce and with the help of fine artisans who ar now creating increasingly refin goods.

By the beginning of the 12t century, Florence becomes republic within the Empire – made up of 12 Consuls, Council of 100 Gentlemen, and Parliament. The city is hence le by nobles, important merchant and major craftsmen.

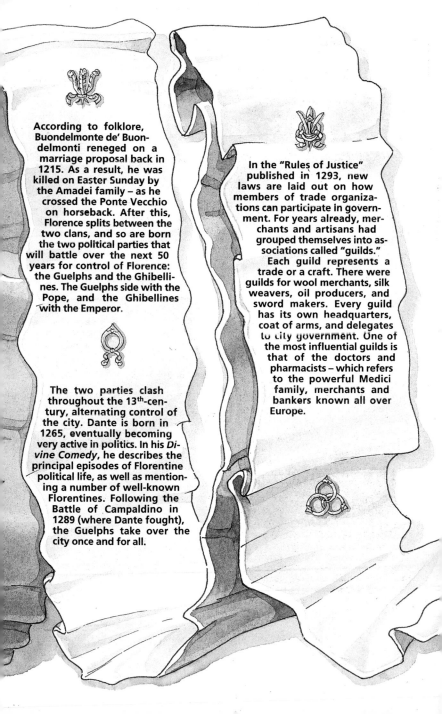

According to folklore, Buondelmonte de' Buondelmonti reneged on a marriage proposal back in 1215. As a result, he was killed on Easter Sunday by the Amadei family – as he crossed the Ponte Vecchio on horseback. After this, Florence splits between the two clans, and so are born the two political parties that will battle over the next 50 years for control of Florence: the Guelphs and the Ghibellines. The Guelphs side with the Pope, and the Ghibellines with the Emperor.

The two parties clash throughout the 13th-century, alternating control of the city. Dante is born in 1265, eventually becoming very active in politics. In his *Divine Comedy*, he describes the principal episodes of Florentine political life, as well as mentioning a number of well-known Florentines. Following the Battle of Campaldino in 1289 (where Dante fought), the Guelphs take over the city once and for all.

In the "Rules of Justice" published in 1293, new laws are laid out on how members of trade organizations can participate in government. For years already, merchants and artisans had grouped themselves into associations called "guilds." Each guild represents a trade or a craft. There were guilds for wool merchants, silk weavers, oil producers, and sword makers. Every guild has its own headquarters, coat of arms, and delegates to city government. One of the most influential guilds is that of the doctors and pharmacists – which refers to the powerful Medici family, merchants and bankers known all over Europe.

In 1434, Cosimo dei Medici – known as Cosimo the Elder – becomes “Gonfalonier of the Republic” after defeating the premier families of Florence. Among these are the Capponi, Strozzi, Albizi, Alberti, and Pitti clans.

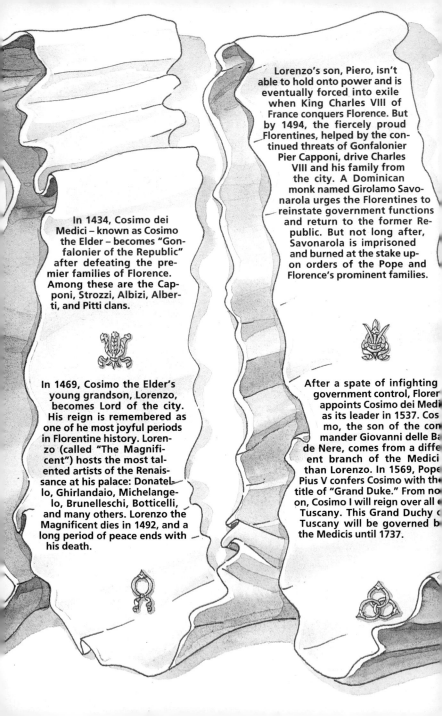

In 1469, Cosimo the Elder’s young grandson, Lorenzo, becomes Lord of the city. His reign is remembered as one of he most joyful periods in Florentine history. Lorenzo (called “The Magnificent”) hosts the most talented artists of the Renaissance at his palace: Donatello, Ghirlandaio, Michelangelo, Brunelleschi, Botticelli, and many others. Lorenzo the Magnificent dies in 1492, and a long period of peace ends with his death.

Lorenzo’s son, Piero, isn’t able to hold onto power and is eventually forced into exile when King Charles VIII of France conquers Florence. But by 1494, the fiercely proud Florentines, helped by the continued threats of Gonfalonier Pier Capponi, drive Charles VIII and his family from the city. A Dominican monk named Girolamo Savonarola urges the Florentines to reinstate government functions and return to the former Republic. But not long after, Savonarola is imprisoned and burned at the stake upon orders of the Pope and Florence’s prominent families.

After a spate of infighting government control, Florer appoints Cosimo dei Medi as its leader in 1537. Cosimo, the son of the con mander Giovanni delle Ba de Nere, comes from a diffe ent branch of the Medici than Lorenzo. In 1569, Pope Pius V confers Cosimo with th title of “Grand Duke.” From no on, Cosimo I will reign over all Tuscany. This Grand Duchy Tuscany will be governed b the Medicis until 1737.

When the last Medici – Gian Gastone – dies, political motives cause the Grand Duchy to be passed to Francesco di Lorena, husband of the Empress of Austria. In 1799, Napoleon sweeps into Italy and kicks the Lorenas from their throne. Only after the Vienna Congress of 1815 are they again allowed to set foot in Florence.

At the close of the Florentine Renaissance, Florence votes to unite with the Kingdom of Italy. The last Grand Duke, Leopoldo II di Lorena (called "Canapone") is forced from the city in 1859 – in a bloodless confrontation.

From 1865 to 1870, Florence is the capital of the new Kingdom of Italy.

During World War II, Florence is occupied by the Nazis. Before they are expelled by the Allied and Resistance forces, the Nazis turn the city's bridges into minefields, blowing all but the Ponte Vecchio to pieces.

Following heavy Autumn rainstorms, the Arno River floods its banks on November 4, 1966. The terrible floods throw the city into chaos and cause enormous damage to the historical center of Florence. But, with the help of young people from all over the world ("mud angels") Florence's artistic and cultural treasures are saved.

In the midst of increased political turbulence, the Mafia plants a very powerful bomb next to the Uffizi Gallery on May 27, 1993. The explosion kills five people after striking violently at the heart of the city, and damages many priceless works of art.

[redacted]ist of itineraries

itinerary 1
Palazzo Medici Riccardi
S. Lorenzo and the Medici Chapels
S. Lorenzo Market
S. Marco
Santissima Annunziata
Galleria dell'Accademia

itinerary 2
[redacted]istery
[redacted]mo (Cathedral)
[redacted]nelleschi's Dome
[redacted]to's Bell Tower
[redacted]seo dell'Opera di S. Maria del Fiore
Loggia del Bigallo
Orsanmichele

itinerary 3
Piazza della Signoria
Loggia dei Lanzi
Palazzo Vecchio
Galleria degli Uffizi
Ponte Vecchio
History of Science Museum

itinerary 4
Piazza S. Croce
S[redacted]Croce
[redacted]rgello
Badia Fiorentina
In the footsteps of Dante...

itinerary 5
Central Station
Piazza S. Maria Novella
S. Maria Novella
S. Trinita
Santi Apostoli
Palazzo Strozzi
Palazzo Davanzati

itinerary 6
Palazzo Pitti
Giardino di Boboli
S. Spirito
Carmine
Museo della Specola

itinerary 7
S. Niccolò
The "Ramps"
Piazzale Michelangelo
S. Miniato
Forte di Belvedere
Arcetri

itinerary 8
FIESOLE
Badia Fiesolana
Piazza Mino da Fiesole
Duomo (Cathedral)
Roman amphitheater
S. Francesco
Scenic tour

itinerary 9
Cascine
Giardino degli Orti Oricellari
Fortezza da Basso
Giardino Stibbert
Giardino dell'Orticoltura
Villa Demidoff

itinerary 1

1. Palazzo Medici Riccardi
2. S. Lorenzo and the Medici Chapels
3. S. Lorenzo Market
4. S. Marco
5. Santissima Annunziata
6. Galleria dell'Accademia

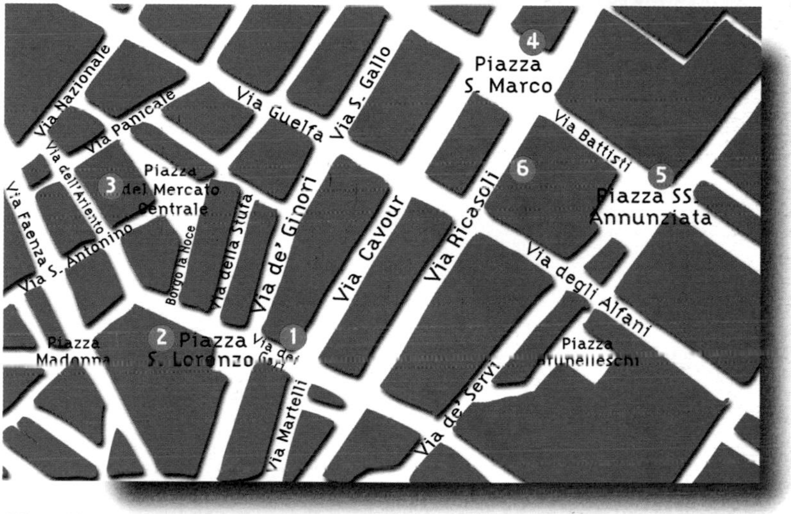

Palazzo Medici Riccardi

Palazzo Medici Riccardi is located at the corner of via Cavour (once called via Larga), and via dei Gori. The palace was built by Michelozzo, a famous architect, upon orders of Cosimo the Elder. The construction work began in 1444 and lasted almost 10 years. The three-story palace is remarkably beautiful with elegant windows on the top floors where Cosimo's son Piero, and Lorenzo the Magnificent lived in plush apartments. The ground floor is covered with large, jutting stones ("bugnato"), while the stones on the top two are lined with much smoother. Cosimo the Elder lived here on the ground floor. He also had a sumptuous chapel, the Cappella dei Magi, erected within the palace as well as courtyards and gardens.

Cappella dei Magi

The floor of the Cappella dei Magi is paved with inlaid marble of many different colors. Above the altar hangs a painting which depicts the birth of Jesus. Winding along the walls, leading up to the masterpiece is a full crowd of knights, noble ladies, and maidens all led by the three wise men (the "Magi"). A beautiful fresco by Benozzo Gozzoli.

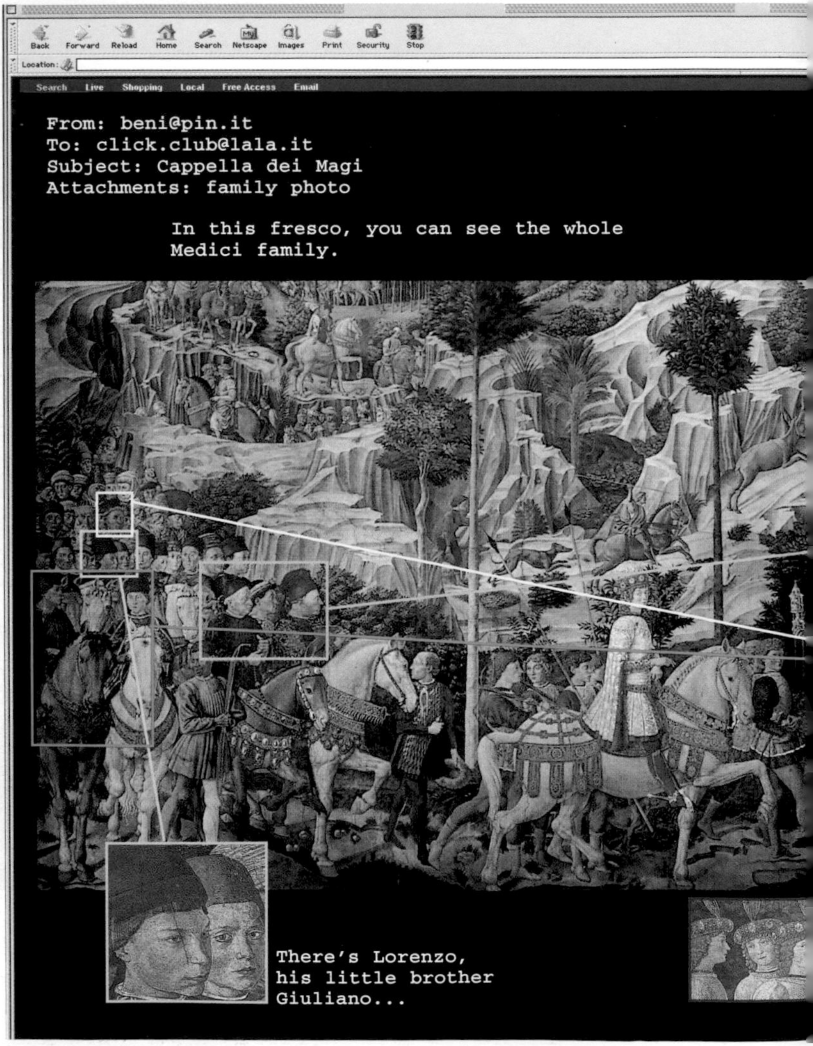

The caravan (*La cavalcata dei Magi*) crosses and descends into a lovely countryside which looks a lot like the landscapes in Tuscany. The characters are dressed in luxurious clothing sewn from precious fabrics embroidered with pure gold. The horses are draped in harnesses reserved for special occasions, as well as bits and stirrups engraved in gold.

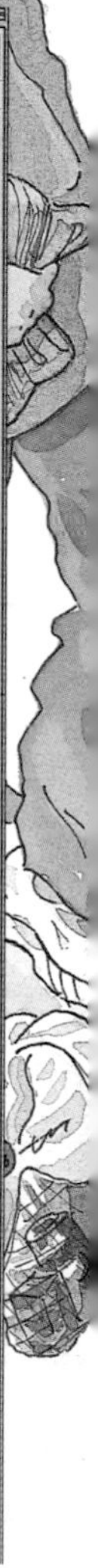

... grandfather Cosimo the Elder and the father Piero "the Gouty" (so called because he had the illness called gout).

There are also the two guests of honor from the May Day party: Galeazzo Maria Sforza and Sigismondo Pandolfo Malatesta.

The painter Benozzo Gozzoli is also in the painting (you can tell it's him because his name is written on his hat).

nd the sisters
aria, Bianca
nd Nannina...

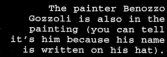

The Medici family lived in this **palace** (1) up until 1540, when the Grand Duke Cosimo I moved into the Palazzo della Signoria. The palace still was owned by the Medicis, however, until 1659 when Grand Duke Ferdinando II sold it to Marquis Gabriello Riccardi for 40,000 scudos. That's why the palace is called Palazzo Medici Riccardi today.

1

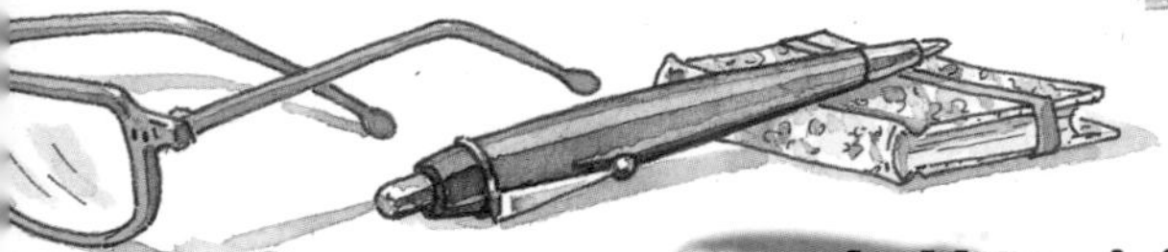

S. Lorenzo and the Medici Chapels

The **Basilica of S. Lorenzo** (2) was erected upon the ruins of an ancient church (from the 11th-century), which was outside the city walls and dedicated to S. Ambrogio. In 1419, at the Medici's expense, the new construction began according to the incomplete plans begun by Filippo Brunelleschi.

2

The church rises above a low flight of steps and has a weird façade made of bricks and stones left rough because the Florentines couldn't agree on a design for the stunning marble façade they'd wanted.

The interior is very big, divided into 3 aisles (naves). There are many works by famous artists like Donatello who sculpted the bronze pulpits (on marble columns) in the middle nave. In the left nave there's a fresco depicting the martyrdom of S. Lorenzo (St. Lawrence). At the center of a curious, busy crowd, you can see the grill on which the saint is stretched, being barbecued by a fire below, fanned by the breath of a person to the left. All the Medici family members are buried here. The tomb of Cosimo the Elder is at the center of the floor in front of the main altar. It is decorated with colored pieces of marble that

form an elegant design. On the left side of the main altar, there's a beautiful inlaid door leading to the Old Sacristy where other Medicis are buried. The Sacristy was created by Brunelleschi. It houses sculptures by Donatello, a frame of terra-cotta statues, cherubs, and a small dome ceiling (cupola) – a fresco of blue representing the evening sky, sprinkled with golden stars that criss-cross in the form of constellations.

To get to the Medici Chapels, pass through Piazza Madonna degli Aldobrandini, around the back of the Basilica. The Medici Chapels include the crypt, the **Chapel of the Princes** (3) and the New Sacristy. Inside the crypt – a large airy space with a vaulted ceiling – the tombs of Medici princes are marked with marble slabs on the floor. The crypt has a passageway where Cosimo the Elder is buried. A stairway leads from the crypt to the magnificent Chapel of the Princes completely covered in semi-precious stones and inlaid marble. Towards the bottom of the walls are the sixteen **coats of arms** (4) of the Grand Duchy of Tuscany – studded with lapis lazuli, mother of pearl, coral and onyx, in an intricate design crossed with red marble from Barga, green from Corsica, and white from Carrara. Following a narrow hall, you reach the New Sacristy, built by Michelangelo. Here you'll find the sepulchers of Lorenzo, Duke of Urbino and Giuliano, Duke of Nemours, the grandson and son respectively of Lorenzo the Magnificent.

Michelangelo's statues decorating the two tombs are absolute-

ly beautiful. In the middle, the Duke of Urbino poses in deep thought on the side, while the Duke of Nemours seems ready for action. Beneath them, four figures recline on the sarcophagus. They represent the passage of time. For the Duke of Urbino, Dawn and Dusk; for the Duke of Nemours, Day and **Night** (1).

1

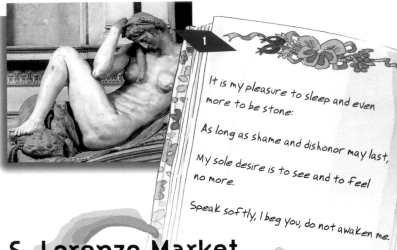

It is my pleasure to sleep and even more to be stone:

As long as shame and dishonor may last,

My sole desire is to see and to feel no more.

Speak softly, I beg you, do not awaken me.

S. Lorenzo Market

From: beni@pin.it
To: sebastiano@lala.it
Subject: e-mail for gourmands
Attachments: market photo

Dear Seba, here I am at the central market in Florence - on a mini-reconnaissance - reconnaissance mission. Huge displays of steaks 4 inches thick (you've got to eat them rare almost bloody!). There's a sign: "Trippa Lampredotto and Budellina of the day" You know what that means? I asked: they say it's got to do with the guts (of the stomach) of the cow and that they are supposed to be delicious in stews or boiled with different sauces. You know what? I think I'll pass! I'd rather dive into a well-cooked pork chop with beans "all'uccelletto" (in tomato sauce). I'll top it all off with a yummy slice of castagnaccio (chestnut cake), but nothing beats your custard pastries...
I'm attaching a picture of the market-shot with a 30 mm lens. And by the way the Castagnaccio recipe isn't bad.
Later, Beniamino

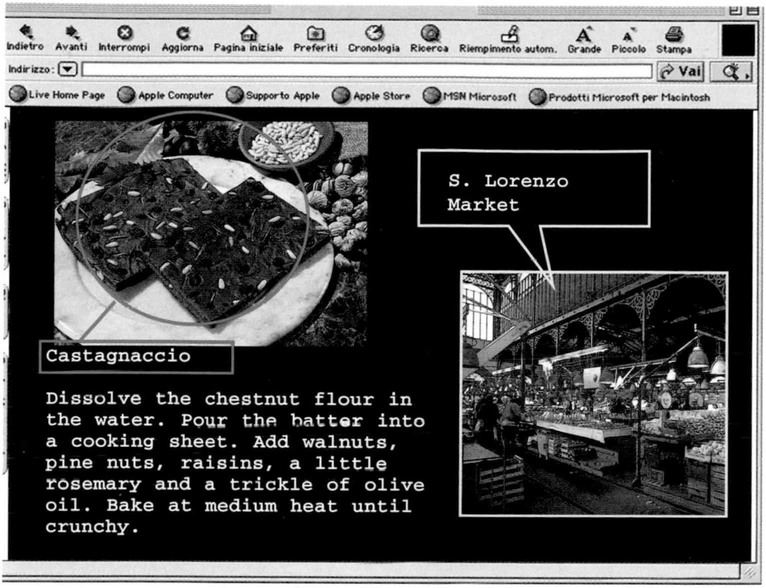

S. Marco

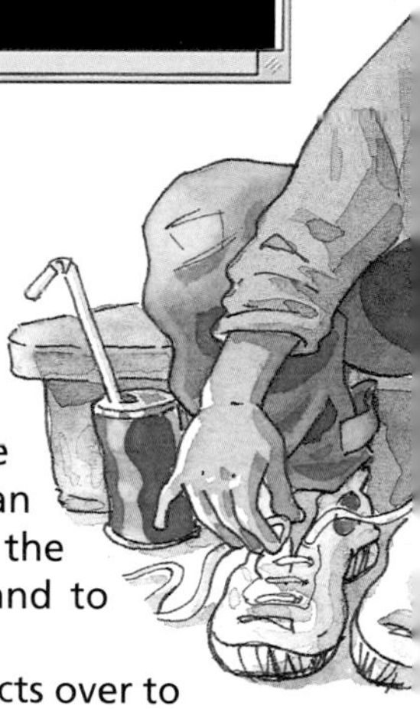

The Convent and Church of S. Marco were built in 1299 above an ancient oratory. The order of monks who used to live there became obsolete, so Cosimo the Elder – with the Pope Eugenio IV – wanted to move the Dominican monks to Fiesole here – both to spruce up the palace that bordered his Via Larga property and to create a home worthy for the friars.
In 1437, Cosimo turned the reconstruction projects over to his favorite architect Michelozzo.
Michelozzo reconstructed the square cloister with their columns and elegant arches. The doors of the church, the chapter house (where the monks met), the refectory and the poorhouse all open onto this courtyard. The monks' cells were up on the next floor. The cells were tiny little bedrooms with a door so low you had to duck your head. Next to the cells, there was a large library where the Dominicans friars could read and study. Brother Antonino, the prior of S. Marco, wanted to add a little something to Michelozzo's work. He asked Cosimo to brighten the white walls with

images from the gospel that highlighted the monks' contemplative life. Giovanni da Fiesole, a monk artist was chosen to paint the convent's frescoes with colorful angels moving with precious robes, vivid wings, and golden halos, and scenes from the life of Jesus. All showcase luminous characters set with the harmonious Tuscan countryside in the background.

After the frescoes were completed, Giovanni was henceforth known as "Beato Angelico" (Blessed and Angelic – "Fra Angelico" –) for the inspiration and beauty reflected in his work.

To see the loveliest frescoes, climb the stairs to the first floor, and right there before your eyes, you'll see the large ***Annunciation*** (1) set in a Renaissance portico next to a flowering garden. Then in the hallway where the first cells face each other, you can see the ***Virgin and Jesus with eight saints*** (2). To identify the saints you need to look at the **symbols** (3) painted by the artist. To the left: St. Dominic (a star over his head), Saints Cosma and Damiano (recognizable because they are brothers with doctor's

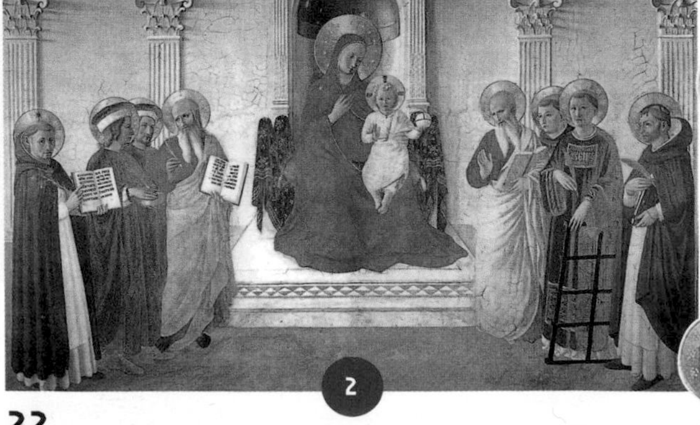

4

hats) and St. Mark the Evangelist (with a book in his hand). On the right: St. John the Evangelist (also with a book in his hand), St. Thomas Aquinas (with a bright star on his habit), St. Lawrence (with his grill) and St. Peter of Verona (with his head bloody from the hatchet that killed him).
The friars' cells have frescoes. To see the most beautiful of these it's best to start from cell 1, where the fresco represents *The appearance of Jesus to Mary Magdalene* in front of his empty tomb, surrounded by the garden full of flowers and plants. In cell 3 there's another lovely *Annunciation*. In cell 7 there's the fresco of ***Christ being mocked*** (4). Jesus blindfolded and wearing a crown of thorns is stricken by images of hands, clubs, spitting, and insults that float in the green background. At his feet, Mary and St. Domenic mourn. Returning to the ground floor, there is a *Crucifixion* large fresco found in the chapter house.
The majestic scene covers an entire wall – with three crosses silhouetted against a reddish sky. Below, the Virgin is supported by the merciful ladies, and surrounded by a host of saints. In the poorhouse – Sala dell'Ospizio dei Pellegrini – you'll find a number of other works by Fra Angelico, painted for other churches in Florence. Immediately on the left is the *Tabernacolo dei Linaioli* (shrine of the flax spinners): an enthroned Madonna surrounded by 12 enchanting **musical angels** (5). The shrine is closed by two wooden panels with the figures of saints. On the other walls in the room there are: a large painting, which hung over the altar of S. Marco church, on the right wall hangs next to the splendid *Last Judgment*, below is the very famous *Deposition from the Cross*, and in front of the entrance, an extraordinary series of small paintings stretches across the wall narrating the life of Christ as a comic strip. The cloister has a tall cedar tree. Underneath the arcade you'll find funerary monuments, coats of arms, and a few frescoes.
Right in front of the entrance to the chapter house there's a large bell (the *Piagnona*) which rang the day the convent was sieged and a very important monk – Girolamo Savonarola – was arrested.

5

Santissima Annunziata

2

The rectangular **square** (1) where the Church of Santissima Annunziata looms is spacious and harmonious. At the center, hovers a **statue** of Grand Duke Ferdinando I dei Medici on horseback. To the side are two odd fountains with bronze see monsters forming the base. Other monsters constitute the central jets which sprew water. All three of these were created in the 17th-century. Especially memorable is the elegant arcade which defines three sides of the square. If we approach from Via de Servi, the church's portico will be right in front of us. To the left is the portico of the Brotherhood of Mary's Servants (also called dei Serviti) and to the right is the Ospedale degli Innocenti (Hospital of the Innocents), built by the great architect Filippo Brunelleschi between 1419 and 1424. This arcade rises up to a flight of steps and its arches are supported by thin stone columns constructed of "pietra serena." The gorgeous decorative roundels are inserted above the columns, between one archway and the next. Made of ceramic these **roundels** (2) were created by Andrea della Robbia, who along with uncle Luca and son Giovanni, was one of the most celebrated painted-terracotta craftsmen of his day. Each of the medallions with sky-blue backgrounds is modeled after a swaddled baby – to underline the building's function. The Ospedale degli Innocenti in fact accepted all newborns abandoned by mothers who couldn't provide for them. Often the women arrived at nighttime leaving their babies wrapped in a blanket on a revolving wheel. They would ring a doorbell, and the nuns would know there was a new arrival. They rotated the wheel and took the child in. The hospital went on like this until 1875. On the left side of the arcade you can still see a tiny square window which houses the famous "wheel of the innocent."

1

The Church of Santissima Annunziata was built in 1250 as a little oratory for the Order of the Serviti. This monastic order had been founded just a few years earlier by 7 Florentine gentlemen who had withdrawn as hermits on

3

Mt. Senario. Between 1444 and 1481, the architect Michelozzo expanded and modified the structure of the church and its cloisters, in particular the Chiostrino dei Voti (Little Cloister of Vows), inspired by the one he'd designed in the Palazzo Medici Riccardi.

Today we see the church transformed with an 18th-century façade of stucco, gold, and marble. Florentines have a soft spot for this church, because they consider it the most appropriate place to ask the Virgin Mary for help. Legend has it that two miracles occurred here – in the 13th-century. While painting a fresco of the *Annunciation* here, the painter Fra Bartolomeo was having a tough time imagining the face of Mary. Try and try again, exhausted, he finally fell asleep. When he woke up he was shocked to find that the Virgin's face had been depicted so splendidly that he thought only an angel could have painted it. Inside the church, you absolutely have to see the decorations on the **little temple of the *Annunciation*** (3), as well as the frescoes in the Chiostrino dei Voti. As you leave, you'll see the entrance to the Archaeological Museum next to the arch in Via della Colonna. It's a fascinating museum with a collection of Egyptian, Etruscan, Greek and Roman artifacts.

...bees

From: beni@pin.it
To: elettra@lala.it
Subject: medium difficulty question for boring math geeks (information courtesy of your know-it-all Japanese friend)
Attachments: photo of bees

Dear Elettra,
try to solve this problem!!!

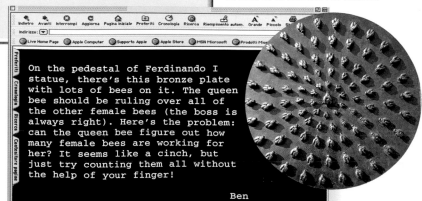

On the pedestal of Ferdinando I statue, there's this bronze plate with lots of bees on it. The queen bee should be ruling over all of the other female bees (the boss is always right). Here's the problem: can the queen bee figure out how many female bees are working for her? It seems like a cinch, but just try counting them all without the help of your finger!

Ben

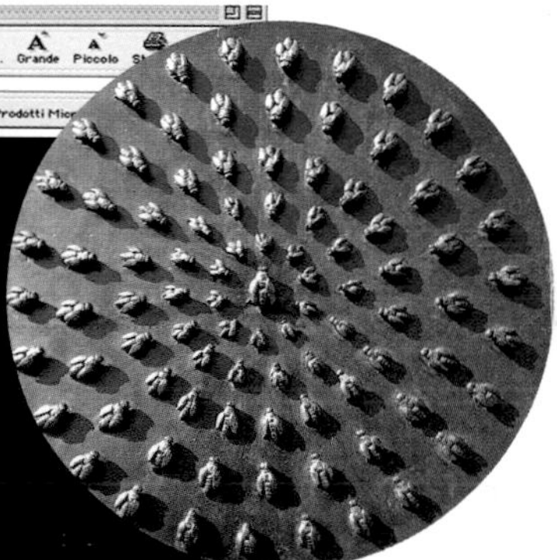

Galleria dell'Accademia

1

Besides finding awesome tapestries and paintings in this museum, you can see some of Mchelangelo's most famous sculptures here. The most famous of all is ***David*** (1). To protect him from bad weather, David was transferred here from Piazza della Signoria where he stood in front of Palazzo Vecchio, as a symbol of freedom for the Florentines. Michelangelo's statue depicts the exact moment when the young David gathered up all his courage to defeat the giant Goliath in a battle that seemed impossible. Despite appearances (the statue is more than 12 feet tall) David was just a young man with an adolescent's body. And the giant Goliath was so enormous, he scared everyone to death.

itinerary 2

1. Baptistery
2. Duomo (Cathedral)
3. Brunelleschi's Dome
4. Giotto's Bell Tower
5. Museo dell'Opera di S. Maria del Fiore
6. Loggia del Bigallo
7. Orsanmichele

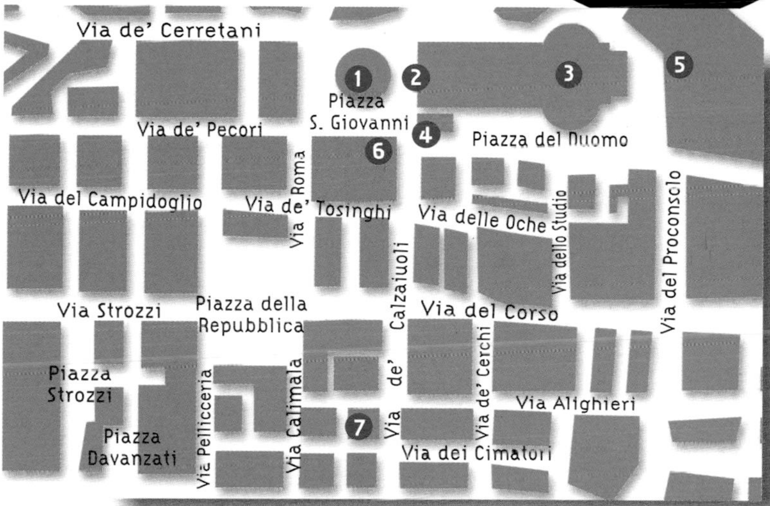

Baptistery

The **Baptistery** (1) is one of the oldest monuments still standing in Florence. It's probably built on the foundation of, and with the same columns, capitals and marble as the ancient Roman praetorium. The Baptistery was rebuilt between the 4th and 5th BC, but what you see now was constructed between the 11th and 12th-centuries when Florence was undergoing an architectural boom. Florentines had hoped this could be their Cathedral honoring St. John the Baptist. It has an octagonal floor plan and is covered in geometric patterns of white marble from the Apuane Mountains and green marble from Prato in the shapes of lines, rectangles, arches, and triangles.

1

1

The eight smooth, white marble segments on the roof form a squished pyramid – topped off with an octagonal lantern (type of "skylight") and a crowning gold ball and cross.
Three sides of the building open with massive doors. The oldest of these is the one to the south (facing the Loggia del Bigallo) made of heavy bronze and decorated with 28 panels. Twenty of these recount the life of St. John the Baptist, and also illustrate the principle virtues of the Church. These doors are the work of sculptor Andrea Pisano, created between 1330 and 1338. On the opposite (north) side, you'll see another awesome set of doors, made by Lorenzo Ghiberti, with the help of artists like Donatello. This door also has 28 panels: 20 illustrate episodes from the New Testament; the other eight introduce the Evangelists and Prophets of the church. On the motif framing the panels, you can see tiny 3-D busts of young an old men. The fifth head from the top in the band at the center of the left door is none other than Ghiberti himself, sporting a weird hat. But the most famous and splendid of all the doors face east towards the Duomo. The doors, also carved by Ghiberti, were considered so fantastic that Michelangelo nicknamed them "**the gates of paradise**"(1). If you look closely, you'll see **ten great moments** (2) from the Old Testament. During World War II, these gates were hidden away to protect them from destruction. When they were finally returned to their proper place, experts decided to clean the grungy dark panels and were shocked to uncover sparkling gold carvings. For years, everyone had assumed these doors were made of bronze since the patina was so dark.
The panels you are looking at now are copies. The originals are protected in the Cathedral's Museum: the Museo dell'Opera di S. Maria del Fiore.

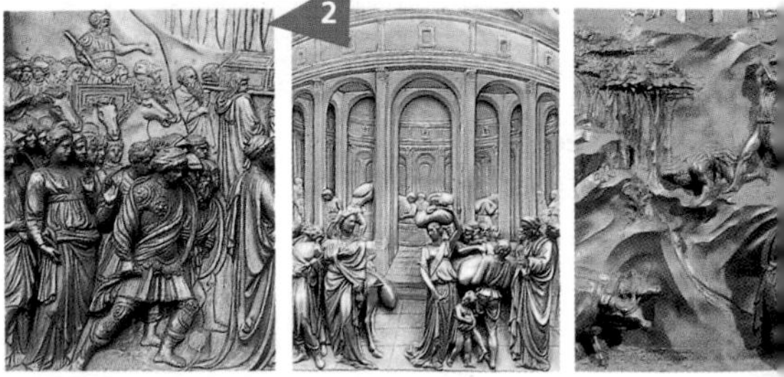

2

The walls on the inside of the Baptistery are inlaid with marble – continuing the geometric motifs on the exterior. You will also see tall columns taken from the Orient, ancient Rome, and the Middle Ages. The floor is breathtaking: its intricate, interlacing designs could fool you into thinking this is an elegant rug. Looking up at the dome there's a **great mosaic** (3) depicting scenes from the lives of Jesus and John the Baptist, and stories from the Old Testament, along with angels prophets, apostles, and a **freaky picture of what hell looks like** (4). These smaller scenes build up to the massive central figure of Christ the Redeemer. These mosaics were a huge undertaking, begun in 1228. Numerous artists collaborated on the project, painting elaborate pasteboards which were then used as outlines for the mosaics. To the right of the entrance, you can see the christening font from 1300. And to the right of the altar you see the beautiful tomb of the antipope Giovanni the 23rd – commissioned by Giovanni di Bicci (father of Cosimo the Elder) and executed by architect Michelozzo and sculptor Donatello. The Medicis, who'd been the Pope's bankers before he was ousted, wanted to honor the memory of this man who died poor and alone in Florence.

3

4

Duomo

In 1293, the Florentines decided to demolish the church of S. Reparata, the city's Cathedral since 1128 (after the Baptistery), and hoped to build a new church that was the biggest and most sumptuous anyone had seen before. Florence needed lots of money for the undertaking though, so really high taxes were imposed. But since the leaders weren't sure everyone in the city was paying up, they put an odd money box (a hollowed-out log) – in the church of S. Reparata with the words "log of your conscience" scrawled on it. It is believed that guilty tax evaders threw in at least some of the money they owed.

The Cathedral project was entrusted to a fabulous architect, Arnolfo di Cambio. Ground was broken on September 8, 1296 and from that moment on, Florentines were fascinated by the ins-and-outs of construction. Legend has it that Dante was one of the most curious voyeurs and had his own special observation seat. That spot is marked nowadays with a plaque known as "Dante's pebble."

Arnolfo died in 1301 – and the work really slowed down after that. The Duomo construction only picked up seriously when master painter Giotto di Bondone took over. Giotto was particularly interested in getting the bell tower built. He passed away in 1337. The bell tower and the cathedral projects were again at a standstill, left unfinished.

From that point on, Francesco Talenti took over as chief designer. But by now, Florentines weren't so sure about Arnolfo's original blueprints and wanted to expand the project. After lots

2

of talking, a group of architects and painters was finally picked to revise the plans. The group constructed a little model of the Duomo which was thorough and detailed enough to serve as a guide for the construction workers. At last, the cathedral was finished in 1421 – a whole 125 years after work had begun! Exactly for that reason, when Florentines want to say something is taking a really long time, they'll exclaim "It's just like building the Duomo!"

The exterior of the **Cathedral** (1) is covered in pink, white, and green marble in designs supposedly completed by Giotto (in the first part near the façade), and Talenti (in the section where the dome-builder Filippo Brunelleschi erected his chapels).

The prettiest of the side doors is the set facing Via de' Servi on the north: the "**almond gates**" (2). They got this name because the Madonna statue above the entrance is inside an oval frame (similar to an almond). Two-thirds of the façade (interrupted by Arnolfo and Talenti) had been left rough and bare. In the 1800s, architect Emilio De Fabris finally finished the façade you now see, crammed with statues and ornamentation that seem a little out of sync with the church's understated sides and apse.

The sparse interior is remarkable because of the height and immensity of the aisles. The Duomo of Florence is in fact the 4th biggest church in the world – behind St. Peter's in Rome, the Cathedral of Milan, and St. Paul's in London. Don't skip over the stained glass window on the façade, designed by Lorenzo Ghiberti, and Paolo Uccello, or the frescoes of **two famous knights** (3) in the left nave. The first by Andrea del Castagno is of Niccolò da Tolentino, the other of Giovanni Acuto, is by Paolo Uccello.

The Duomo is called S. Maria del Fiore (St. Mary of the Flower).

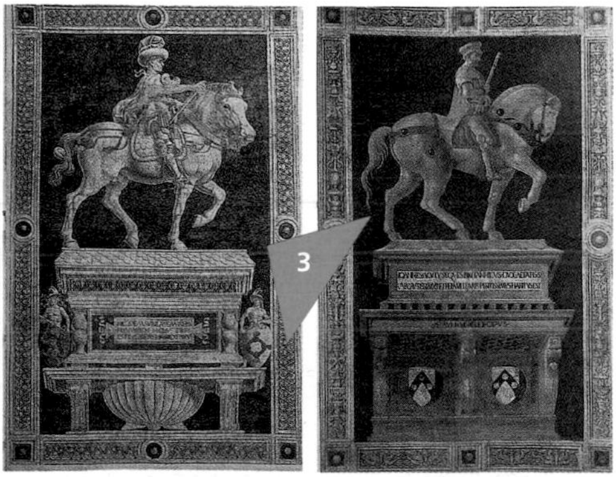

3

From:Beni@pin.it
To:mattia@lala.it
Subject: hobo update
Attachment: photo of the Duomo façade

Dear Mattia, I was picking out lenses and figuring out frames and depths-of-field for a picture of the Duomo square - when all of a sudden, a certain Mr. Vincenzo Bertelli (occupation: hobo) stepped into the picture. He lives by the Loggia del Bigallo. We went over and sat down on the Loggia's steps and started talking about photography. He wanted to know all about my equipment and asked my advice on the best brands, prices, and special functions. He also asked about lenses, especially interested in the under-water one. Pretty random!
But, in exchange he told me a really old story: when the Duomo's façade was still unfinished, the embarrassed Florentines got creative whenever popes, kings, queens, princes, and ambassadors visited. To avoid looking like losers they hung these enormous curtains over the façade - painted specially to fit different occasions. I'm sending you a copy of the façade - try and do something cool with it!

Ben

Brunelleschi's Dome

The original plans for S. Maria del Fiore (St. Mary of the Flower) included a **dome** (1), but no one had any clue how to build it – because, like everything else – it was supposed to be enormous. A public contest was announced in 1418 to figure out a solution. Architects, painters, sculptors, and other maestros all thought they had an answer. Some wanted to built a wooden frame, others wanted to use light pebbles like pumice, some wanted to use concrete. And there was one really odd sugges-

tion: it had to do with building a mountain of dirt mixed with gold coins – piled in the shaped of the dome. The workers would build up the construction as usual. And the dirt? All the locals who wanted to find the money would haul it away for free. In the end however, Filippo Brunelleschi won the contest. The architect had the most original and technically complicated plan – one where the dome would be supported entirely throughout all phases of construction. In 1434, the dome was completed. All that was missing was the **lantern** (a kind of skylight on top) (2). Brunelleschi also designed this, beginning in 1445. The laborers who had to work up on the lantern were exposed to wind and bad weather – and obviously got hungry once in a while. Since it was understandably tough to get down for lunch, the legend goes that Brunelleschi built a kitchen up there where they could eat and drink!

In 1446 the master architect died, never having seen his masterpiece completed. Brunelleschi's dome is still considered one of the most brilliant architectural feats of all time. It's 320 feet high and is 168 feet in diameter.

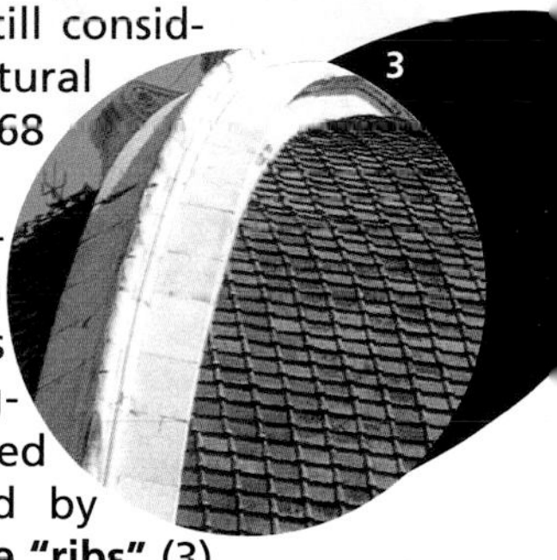

It rests on a marble-lined drum (a tall foundation with 8 sides) with windows like big round eyes. The dome is divided into 8 segments covered in red brick and separated by **enormous white marble "ribs"** (3).

In the 16th-century the dome's interior was completely frescoed by two important painters: Giorgio Vasari and Federico Zuccari. The "cupolone" – as the colorful mega-dome is called – is the first thing you see when you arrive in Florence: the landmark in its skyline and the perfect center point for the city.

Giotto's Bell Tower

In 1334, Giotto took over the chief architect position of the "S. Maria del Fiore workshop." But he had nothing to do with Arnolfo's plans for the cathedral and preferred to concentrate 100 percent on building a new project: the **bell tower** (1). He designed a slender tower covered with colorful marble, intricate carvings, and **decorative panels** (2).

The bell tower has a robust square base, but as you look up the structure seems to get lighter – thanks to increasingly spacious arched windows (double on the middle and triple on the top).

When Giotto died, Andrea Pisano took over the work. Pisano finished sculpting the panels Giotto had designed. But he didn't last until the end either. When he died, Francesco Talenti filled in and finished the job. The bell tower is about 255 feet tall and about 44 feet wide. You can walk up to the roof patio by climbing a staircase with 414 steps.

From up high, you will get a marvelous panorama of the city (even if the dome is so close and huge, you might get a little freaked out).

1

2

Museo dell'Opera di S. Maria del Fiore

3

In Piazza del Duomo, behind the Cathedral, you'll find the Museo dell'Opera di S. Maria del Fiore, which houses sculptures, bas-reliefs, gold, and embroidery – all from the Cathedral.

A magnificent **Pietà** (3) by Michelangelo is on display, in addition to two charming choir stalls. There's a silver altar decorated with gold and enamel, and a moving wooden statue of Mary Magdalene by Donatello (both from the Baptistery).

The museum also has the authentic Andrea Pisano tiles. (The ones lining the bottom of the bell tower are copies).

4

Two Donatello statues from the bell tower can be found here: one of prophet Jeremiah, the other of prophet Habakkuk – called the "Zuccone" (big pumpkin).

An entire room is dedicated to the designs and **architectural models** (4) used to build the Cathedral.

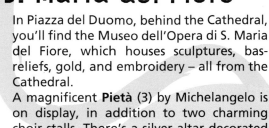

Loggia del Bigallo

5

On the corner of Via Calzaioli, in front of the Baptistery, you'll see an elegant little building, the **Loggia del Bigallo** (5). This was a hospital that took in orphans or abandoned and lost children – built by Alberto Arnoldi for the Compagnia della Misericordia (Brotherhood of Mercy) in the 14th century.

From: mattia@lala.it
To: beni@pin.it
Subject: immediate response
Attachment: photo of Duomo façade

Dear Ben, what do you think about these 3 new façades of the Duomo. Do you think they'd be appropriate?

Mattia

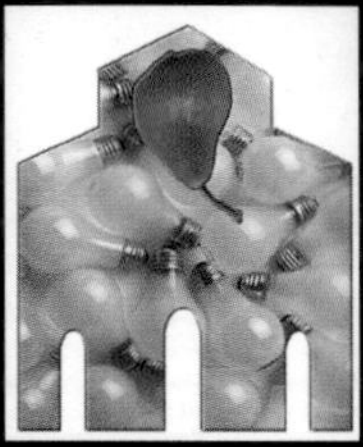

Orsanmichele

Along Via Calzaioli, walking between Piazza del Duomo toward Piazza della Signoria – down the famous Via Calzaioli, you'll run into a strange square building on your right.

This is **Orsanmichele** (1), the most authentic Florentine site in town. To understand this place let's start from the beginning. Its name Orsanmichele is the abbreviation for "Orto di San Michele" (St. Michael's garden). Indeed, this was a church with a garden dedicated to St. Michael here in ancient times. In the 13th-century a "loggia" (open arcade) for a wheat market was built on this garden, prime real estate in downtown Florence. But a fire destroyed the loggia in 1304. In 1336 three architects built a bigger and better arcade where a lot of negotiating, buying and selling went on. A few years down thr road, two other levels were built on top of the loggia. Here Florentines

From: beni@pin.it
To: mattia@lala.it
Subject: out of whack day!
Attachment: panorama picture

Mattia: I printed out the façades and will give them to Bertelli tomorrow. I don't know if he will like them. He's pretty conservative.
Anyways I have other problems today. My favorite glasses (the square blue ones) blew away while I was up on the dome and this is all I could see

Bye Ben (bummed out)

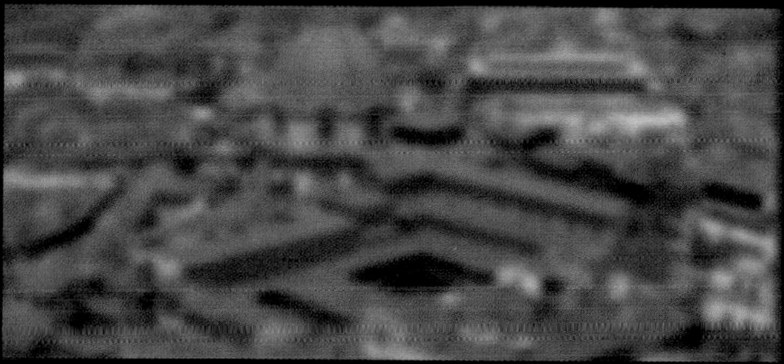

stored grain in case of emergencies – like attacks or famines. So Orsanmichele effectively became a warehouse – a huge silo – in the middle of the city. At the end of the 14th-century the market was moved. The open-air loggia was then closed in with thin stone walls, and transformed into a church. Here, Andrea Orcagna built a splendid shrine to the Virgin Mary. Orsanmichele, with its double duty as a warehouse and a church, become the ideal place for the church of the guilds.

The guilds were groups of Florentine artisans who divided themselves by trades into groups to support and protect their interests (like labor unions today). The following were all in guilds: wool and silk merchants, shoemakers, woodworkers, doctors and pharmacists, oil and sausage makers, blacksmiths and textile merchants, butchers, wine makers and many others. Each guild erected marble **shrines** (1) with statues of its patron saint on pillars outside the old loggia. It was a time of great activity and competition, because the guilds commissioned the most talented artists of the day to sculpt the statues. There are fourteen shrines built into the outside of the church.

On the side facing Via Calzaioli, the following shrines are particularly stunning: Lorenzo Ghiberti's St. John the Baptist on the left (patron saint of the textile merchants), and on the far right, Giambologna's St. Luke (patron saint of judges and notaries). If you turn onto Via Orsanmichele, you'll see two statues by Donatello: St. Peter (patron saint of butchers) and, on the far right **St. George** (2) (patron saint of armorers) – the original is in the Bargello Museum. On Via dell'Arte della Lana, the last shrine on the right was created by Nanni di Banco: of St. Eligius, patron saint of the blacksmiths. On Via dei Lamberti at the far right you can see the statue of St. John the Evangelist by Baccio da Montelupo (patron saint of goldsmiths and silk merchants).

On the outside walls, you can see the symbols of the guilds, some of which were crafted by Luca and Andrea della Robbia, famous for their painted ceramics.

2

itinerary 3

1. Piazza della Signoria
2. Loggia dei Lanzi
3. Palazzo Vecchio
4. Galleria degli Uffizi
5. Ponte Vecchio
6. History of Science Museum

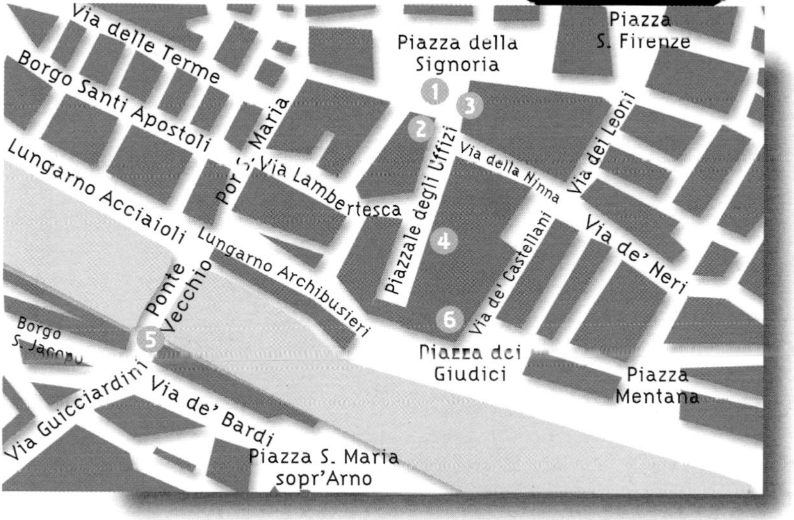

Piazza della Signoria

Piazza della Signoria is one of Italy's most beautiful squares. It was built at the end of the 13th-century when the Guelphs took over Florence and kicked out the Ghibellines once and for all. But as a last slap in the face the homes of the Uberti families and other rebel Ghibellines were torn down. In their place, the Guelphs wanted to build the headquarters of city government. But not wanting the new palace to be erected on "cursed" ground, officials decided to build on the site where the Foraboschi family's homes stood – in particular, their Torre della Vacca (Tower of the Cow). In the centuries that followed, the square's homes, towers, the Church of S. Cecilia, and the Loggia dei Pisani (so called because it was built by Pisan prisoners in 1362), were all destroyed.

If you look beyond the Palazzo Vecchio, there are a few very old buildings facing the square. Among these are the 16th-century **Palazzo Uguccioni** at no. 7, 14th-century **Palazzo della Mercanzia** (1) at no. 10. The latter was the headquarters of a court responsible for resolving disputes between merchants and artisans. This court formed by 6 Florentine and 6 foreign judges was so important that merchants from all over Europe sought justice here. The building is decorated beneath the cornice with the coats of arms of all the city's guilds. On the right side of the square (when you're facing Palazzo Vecchio), you see the wonderful Loggia dei Lanzi.

1

There are a number of statues livening up Piazza della Signoria: the monument of Cosimo I on horseback (the twin of the one in Piazza Santissima Annunziata); the Neptune's fountain (called "Biancone" – the great white one – by Florentines for the enormous out-of-proportion white body of the God of sea).
On the steps of the Palazzo Vecchio there's *Hercules and Caco* ensemble, in addition to copies of the super-famous *Judith* by Donatello and *David* by Michelangelo.
In front of Neptune's fountain, there's a bronze plaque on the pavement which marks the spot where Girolamo Savonarola and two of his followers were burned at the stake as heretics.

Loggia dei Lanzi

2

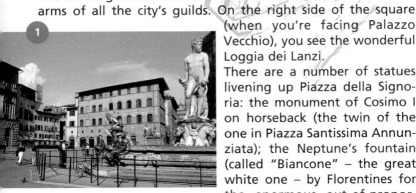

Loggia dei Lanzi (2) was built at the end of the 14th-century for public assemblies of the Signoria (city government). Its name, however, comes from the lansquenets ("lanzi") – the German soldiers stationed here to protect Cosimo I. It's a beautiful structure, with wide decorated arcades, within which there's an old "outdoor museum". Here you'll see the statues of some Roman matriarchs, *Menelaus supporting the body of Patroclus* (a copy of the original Greek work), the *Rape of the Sabine Women*, and Giambologna's statue of *Hercules battling the Centaur*. But the most renowned of all is ***Perseus*** (3), holding up the decapitated head of Medusa. The magnificent statue was crafted by the exquisite goldsmith and sculptor Benvenuto Cellini. Look closely: he signed his name on the hero's belt and shoulder strap.

3

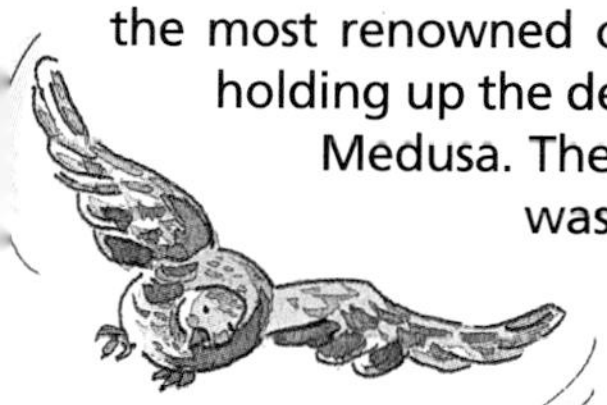

Palazzo Vecchio

Palazzo Vecchio (4) was built between 1299 and 1314 according to the plans of Arnolfo di Cambio. It's a massive stone construction which looks almost like an imposing square fort. On the top edges, you see the flat-topped crenellations of the Guelphs. The Torre di Arnolfo (over 280 feet high) rises up, however with Ghibelline crenellations, that look like swallows' tails. At the top of the tower there's a gold lion rampart. Like the lily, the lion is a symbol of Florence. At the base of

4

1

the tower, there's a big clock which has functioned perfectly since the 17th-century. The government of Florence formed by the gonfalonier and priors moved here at the start of the 14th-century, leaving their old headquarters at the Torre della Castagna (Chestnut Tower) over the Badia (Abbey). The new palace was ideal for the priors, who couldn't leave the building at all during their two month terms. Florentines wanted to make sure their leaders were not distracted by personal or business matters; the priors comfort and security was ensured within these walls.
The palace was expanded in the centuries to come. What we see today is exactly what you would have seen in the 16th century. From the front doors, you walk into a small atrium encircling Verrocchio's fountain of a jumping **bronze cherub** (1). The walls are frescoed, and the columns are adorned with stucco work and gold.
To the left of the atrium, you can find the Sala d'Armi (weapons hall), unchanged since Medieval times when this was the guards' headquarters.
Between the first atrium and the one called the Dogana (Customs), there are two grand staircases, one on the right and on the left. The one on the left leads to the Salone dei Duecento (the hall of 200, a magnificent room where the city council meets today). This hall has a great breathtaking ceiling of inlaid and colored wood made by Benedetto da Maiano. The stairwell on the right leads to the **Salone dei Cinquecento** (Hall of 500) (2), an immense space with a very high ceiling covered with gilted wood ornaments and painted with scenes from the history of Florence.

2

There were originally frescoed by Leonardo da Vinci and Michelangelo along the walls. Leonardo was supposed to use a brand new technique to paint the *Battle of Anghiari*. And not to be outshone, Michelangelo was to paint the *Battle of Cascina*. But neither project was completed. Today the paintings you see along the walls are by Giorgio Vasari.

When Florence was the capital of the Kingdom of Italy between 1865 and 1871 the 500 members of the nation's Parliament met here. Hence the name "500."

In 1540, Cosimo I dei Medici moved out of his palace in Via Larga and set up house here with his wife Eleonora di Toledo, their children, and the whole court. At that time, a huge part of the palace was restored. You can visit these Grand Ducal apartments today. Some of the prettiest rooms are: the wardrobe room, Francesco I's study, the Sala dei gigli (Hall of lilies), with a rich blue ceiling with inlaid gold lilies. The wardrobe is not exactly what you'd expect of a room filled with clothes closets; it is more like a tribute to voyages and adventure. As a matter of fact, the big wood armoires are covered with 57 maps from the 16th-century, with naval routes to faraway lands. In the middle of the room, there's an immense globe, the biggest of its day.

In Palazzo Vecchio there's also a children museum with 5 different laboratories where you can have a good time building, playing, acting, doing experiments, etc.

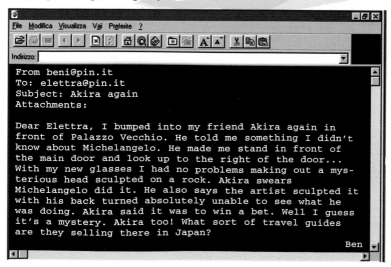

File Modifica Visualizza Vai Preferite ?

Indirizzo:

From beni@pin.it
To: elettra@pin.it
Subject: Akira again
Attachments:

Dear Elettra, I bumped into my friend Akira again in front of Palazzo Vecchio. He told me something I didn't know about Michelangelo. He made me stand in front of the main door and look up to the right of the door... With my new glasses I had no problems making out a mysterious head sculpted on a rock. Akira swears Michelangelo did it. He also says the artist sculpted it with his back turned absolutely unable to see what he was doing. Akira said it was to win a bet. Well I guess it's a mystery. Akira too! What sort of travel guides are they selling there in Japan?

Ben

Galleria degli Uffizi

1

The **Palazzo degli Uffizi** (1) was built at the end of the 16th-century according to the designs of the architect Giorgio Vasari as a center for Florence's administrative offices, archives and courts. At first the Uffizi also included the Medici Theater, a little foundry, and a pharmacy where perfumes, medicines (and sometimes even poisons) were often prepared.
The complex includes two facing buildings. These structures stretch from the Arno river to Piazza della Signoria square, forming a **long narrow square** (2) in the middle.
Inside the palace, you'll find the Uffizi Gallery – the oldest and most famous public art museum in the world. It was Cosimo I's idea to gather the Medici's entire art collection into one place, but it was his son Francesco I who made that dream a reality.
The Medici family's successors, the Lorenas, also played a big part in creating the museum's huge collection you see now.
In 1737, the last Medici heir, Anna Maria Luisa, left the whole priceless collection to the city so Florence could enjoy the art forever.

2

3

Visiting the Uffizi Gallery is a magical experience. Climb a magnificent staircase up to the second floor. Here you'll see the rooms crammed with paintings. The first works hail from the 13th-century and are almost all sacred in subject. Enormous Madonnas, large crucifixions, backdrops of luminous gold. Among these masterpieces, you'll find Giotto's ***Madonna d'Ognissanti*** (3) (Our Lady of All Saints) a huge canvas of the Virgin Mary and child seated on a throne and attended by angels and saints. This type of depiction of Mary enthroned is called a "Maestà" (Majesty).

In the next room you will see the ***Annunciation*** (4) by a Sienese painter, Simone Martini. Here the young Mary is shy and fearful in the sweet angel's presence. He announces the good news with a green branch in his hand. The angel has gorgeous wings and an **odd checkered cape** (5).

4

5

1

Continuing past the beautiful 14th-century paintings, a weird landscape might catch your attention: boats in the foreground, with mountains, trees, and lots of men and animals all over the place. These are monks you see, and the painting depicts hermits in their humble abode while performing their simple day-to-day activities (fishing, praying, painting, and so on). This painting is of a place in Egypt, where the devout would withdraw into solitude: ***Tebaide*** (Thebaid) (1).

After tons of Madonnas, Saints, Adorations, and Annunciations, finally here's a real battle. You see it all in Paolo Uccello's beautiful ***Battaglia di S. Romano*** (Battle of St. Romano) (2): spears, horses, dead guys, trumpets, flags, and warriors with helmets and armor.

2

You'll keep crossing more rooms overflowing with paintings by really famous artists, until you stumble into an especially majestic hall. Two enormous paintings immediately command your attention: ***La nascita di Venere*** (The Birth of Venus) (3) and ***La Primavera*** (Spring) (4), both by Sandro Botticelli. In the first painting, Venus is born from the sea like a pearl. A dainty maiden rushes to wrap here in a cape, while the winds blow her hair about. In the second, the female embodiment of Spring, dressed in flowers, walks barefoot across a meadow of blossoms. She is surrounded by characters that symbolize the joy of this time of years.

3

4

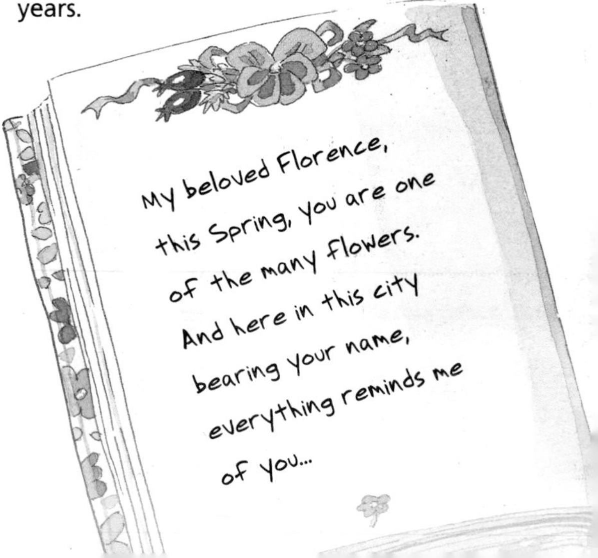
My beloved Florence,
this Spring, you are one
of the many flowers.
And here in this city
bearing your name,
everything reminds me
of you...

1

Close to this magnificent hall of Botticelli paintings is the room dedicated to the genius "par excellence" Leonardo da Vinci. Don't miss his wonderful ***Annunciation*** (1), so elegant, so "frozen in time," and so different from the earlier one by Simone Martini. Now, go into the interesting octagon-shaped Sala della Tribuna ("Gallery room") – where a number of paintings hang from the walls draped in red damask. Among the pictures there are a few portraits of the Medici children: ***Giovanni with a goldfinch*** (2); ***Bia*** (3) dressed in an elegant ballgown; and ***Giovanni*** again (now a little older) ***with his mom Eleonora di Toledo*** (4). There are a number of historical statues in the "Tribuna" – as you also see throughout the wide, long halls with the huge windows overlooking the courtyard. Try and find the funny marble boar that the locals call "**porcellino**" (little piggy) (5). See if you can also find Laocöon and his sons trying to free themselves from the Hydra.

2

3

4

5

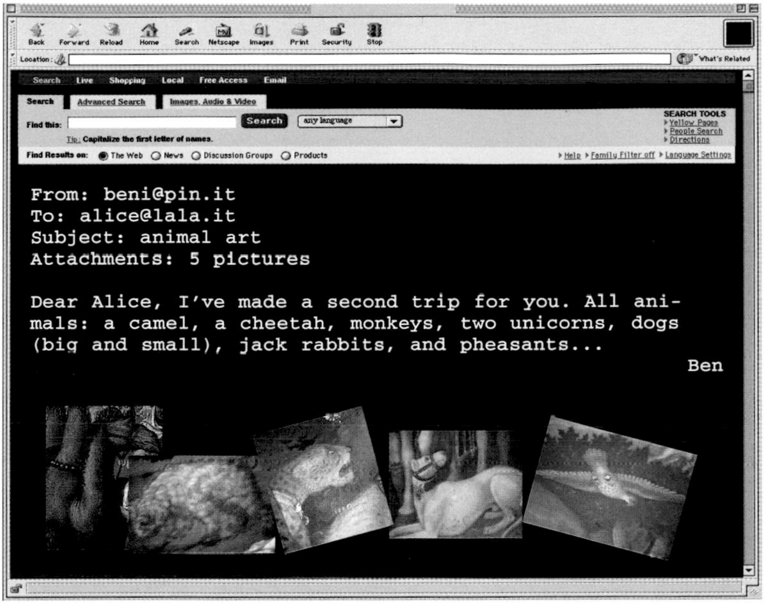

There are three obligatory stops in the rooms to come (full of non-Italian masterpieces as well). Right in front of you, you'll see the ***Round Doni*** (6) painting by Michelangelo. This depiction of the Holy Family once belonged to the Doni family – hence the name. The second one to see is the self-portrait of ***Young Raphael*** (7) – so serious and pensive!

7

The third painting that deserves special mention is ***Bacco Adolescente*** (Bacchus as an Adolescent) (8) by Caravaggio, where the young man wears a wreath of grape leaves, holding an elegant wine goblet and a bunch of Autumn fruit.

6

8

Ponte Vecchio

The **Ponte Vecchio** (Old Bridge) is the oldest bridge in Florence. Once upon a time at the narrowest point on the Arno, the ancient Romans built a bridge of stone and wood as part of the Via Cassia road leading back to Rome. In the 12th-century, the Arno swelled its banks, sweeping away and demolishing the bridge. The Florentines rebuilt it entirely of stone, but in 1333, the river tore it down yet again. In 1345, the bridge was reconstructed again – with a super-solid structure this time – much like what we see today. Even back then, it was packed with little shops – all butcheries – up until 1594 that is. That's when Grand Duke Ferdinando I decided the bridge had gotten too nasty (not to mention smelly) and kicked the 48 meat cutters out, substituting goldsmiths in their place. Everything was spruced up, and the place became much more organized. Each goldsmith had a small house with a display window and a workshop in the back for making jewelry. Ferdinando also had the idea to pick a single (lucky) "renaiolo," or sand digger, to scour the river for the precious "waste" of gems

and gold discarded by the craftsmen. At the center of the bridge you'll see the bust of one of Florence's greatest goldsmiths ever: Benvenuto Cellini. The Ponte Vecchio risked crumbling once again back in 1944 when the German Nazis occupying Florence decided to destroy all the city's bridges in order to slow the Allies down – and have more time to retreat. But at the last minute they decided to blow up all the houses in the streets at either end – thereby sparing the bridge.

The Corridoio Vasariano (Vasari's Hallway) runs up above the workshops on one side of the bridge. This is a long tunnel that Grand Duke Cosimo I had built so he could walk from the Palazzo Vecchio to the royal palace, the Palazzo Pitti – without ever having to go down in the streets. Inside the Corridoio Vasariano there is a vast collection of self-portraits by the greatest painters of all time.

History of Science Museum

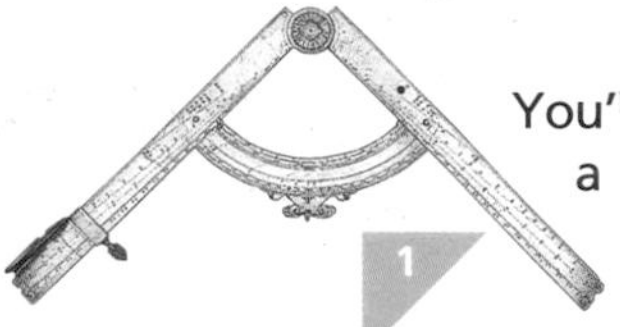

1

You'll find the History of Science Museum in a building along the Arno – close to the Uffizi. This is a place you really should not miss. Its wonderful scientific collection tells the story of science in Florence from the Renaissance through the end of the 19th-century. And it's not too shabby a history either! Galileo Galilei lived and worked in this city – and is considered the father of modern scientific experimentation. The museum has 21 rooms – each focusing on a different subject. You'll find everything from mathematical, mechanical, magnetic, electromagnetic, and surgical instruments to lenses, small **telescopes** (3) and scales. The coolest room is the one dedicated to Galileo. You can examine his famous telescope, **application of the pendulum** (2), **military drawing compass** (1), and an inclined plane used for studying gravity, among other things. The room focusing on the Accademia del Cimento (Experiment Society) is also fascinating. This was an association of scientists, craftsmen, and hobbyists who would meet to conduct experiments. They performed tests on sound, vacuums, heat, and ice – so there are really neat **beakers** (4) and thermometers to look at. Try to make it to the modern chemistry room too. There's a magnificent old chemistry bench used by Grand Duke Pietro Leopoldo for his own personal science projects. End your tour with a thrilling visit to the Planetarium on the top floor.

2

4

3

itinerary 4

1. Piazza S. Croce
2. S. Croce
3. Bargello
4. Badia Fiorentina
5. In the footsteps... of Dante

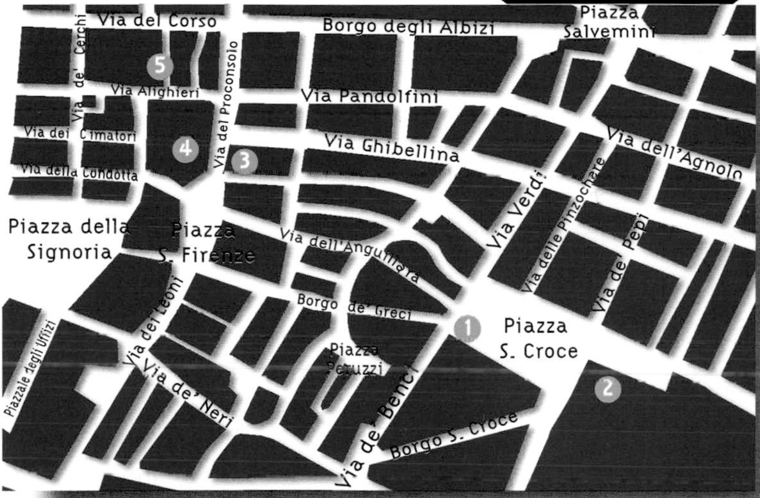

Piazza S. Croce

At the end of the 13th-century there were two major convents outside the city walls. One was S. Maria Novella, where Dominican monks spent their time spreading the Gospel through their writings and studies. Franciscan friars, dedicated to spreading the Gospel through good works, and the example of simplicity and humility set by St. Francis occupied the other, S. Croce. These two monasteries, constructed around their respective churches, both had immense green yards in front of them – important for preaching to the masses. A new city wall was erected in 1284, and the convent of S. Croce now fit within these new urban boundaries. From that point on, the square in front of the church became a social hub. Full of new palaces and shops, it was

the ideal place to meet up with friends, hold festivals, and play sports. Speaking of sports... Even today, the popular "Calcio in Costume" (Historical Soccer) game takes place every June in this **square** (1). There are four teams – determined by the four historical neighborhoods of the city. The Blue team is from S. Croce; the White team from S. Spirito; the Red team is from S. Maria Novella; and the Green team hails from S. Giovanni. It's much more aggressive and no-holds-barred than the soccer matches we watch today. It is closer to rugby or NFL football. Before the game, there's a historic parade where the team members walk through the streets in Renaissance costumes. Strolling along with the players are musicians, flag wavers, and "nobles" on horseback. And at the end of the procession – the prize: a white Tuscan "chianina" cow – all decked out in a frilly get-up.

1

S. Croce

The Basilica of S. Croce was built in 1294 according to the architectural plans of Arnolfo di Cambio. But the Franciscans had already been living on this site for a long time – in an ancient little church they'd expanded and transformed into a monastery. Back then, this area was swampy and gloomy – vulnerable to the Arno's frequent flooding. At that time, the river had two branches – and this area formed a kind of island. This neighborhood was where the city's poorest people lived and worked: that part of the population closest to the Franciscans' hearts. The church soon became an important center where the monks would take in anyone that knocked on their door. When

Arnolfo presented the brothers with his grandiose plans for the basilica, they wanted to ensure that the church would be more than just a refuge for the poor. They hoped the immense edifice might serve as a space for teaching and reflecting upon the stories of the Bible. So, they decided to line the walls with frescoes telling these tales. The project was designed and painted by the era's most prominent artists – and became a real "Bible for the poor."

Unfortunately, you can't see these frescoes any longer (you can only make out a small trace along the left aisle). They were horribly damaged by these frequent floods and were plastered with lime in the 16th-century. Nonetheless, there is still a treasure trove of 14th-century paintings to be seen here.

S. Croce – like a number of other Florentine churches – stood for centuries with an unfinished façade of rough stone. In the 19th-century, the city decided to cover it with colorful marble and to add the slender bell tower.

If you look up when you enter the church, the first impression you'll probably have is just how huge the place is, and how much light filters in from the **windows above the nave arches** (2). If you keep walking and look down, you can't miss all the **tombstones** (3) on the floor: there are a whopping 276 of them! As a matter of fact, many Florentines wanted to be buried in this very church. The wealthiest among them built elaborate chapels for their entire families – complete

2

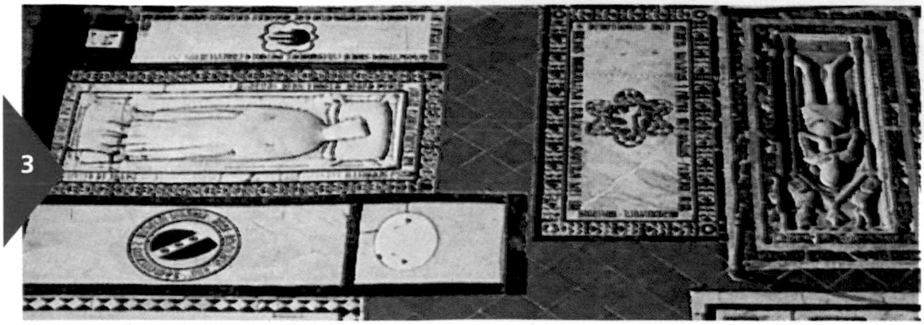
3

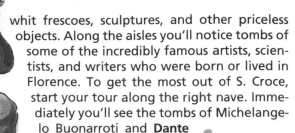

whit frescoes, sculptures, and other priceless objects. Along the aisles you'll notice tombs of some of the incredibly famous artists, scientists, and writers who were born or lived in Florence. To get the most out of S. Croce, start your tour along the right nave. Immediately you'll see the tombs of Michelangelo Buonarroti and **Dante Alighieri** (1). Well, Dante's is actually a "cenotaph" – an empty tomb. His body never made it back to Florence, the city that had sent him into exile. A little farther down, there's a lovely pulpit sculpted by Benedetto da Maiano. Then there are two more tombs, both of famous writers: **Vittorio Alfieri** (2) and Niccolò Machiavelli. After these, you should take a look at Donatello's splendid ***Annunciation* shrine** (3), made of pietra serena – and inlaid with solid gold.

1

2

Walking on, you'll see two more tombs, of the composer Gioachino Rossini and poet **Ugo Foscolo** (4) – who once wrote a poem called *Sepulchers* where he talked about this exact church and all the illustrious Italians who were to be buried here.

Among the many chapels at the end of the nave, the loveliest are the ones with the frescoes by Giotto (to the right of the main altar). The Peruzzi Chapel illustrates *Stories from the lives of St. John the Baptist and other saints*. The Bardi Chapel shows *Scenes of St.*

4

3

Francis's life. Take a close look at the faces of the monks during the moment when **St. Francis dies** (5) – they are very moving. The other chapels also have exceptional paintings. There are works created by the school of Giotto: Taddeo Gaddi, his son Agnolo, and Maso di Banco.

Now take a look at Donatello's **Crucifixion** (6) – which spurred an intense debate between the artist and the architect Filippo Brunelleschi. Brunelleschi thought Donatello's rendering of Jesus looked too much like a simple peasant – too human and not nearly divine enough. The Crucifixion is located in the chapel on the far left; it hangs above the altar. Returning up the left nave, there are a few more noteworthy monuments: those of the musician Luigi Cherubini and the great scientist **Galileo Galilei** (7).

Back Forward Reload Home Search Netscape Images Print Security Stop

Location:

Search Live Shopping Local Free Access Email

From: beni@pin.it
To: clickclub@lala.it
Subject: flood of 1966
Attachments: photos of Florence under-water and Cimabue's *Crucifixion*

Right after I walked into S. Croce - all my cameras, backpacks, extra glasses, and notepad in tow - I went and slipped on this totally worn-out slab of stone. I made a huge thud and all my stuff fell on what I found out was a knight's tomb...
Before I knew it, a monk had shot over like a lightning bolt and picked everything up. From that moment on, Brother Gregorio wouldn't let me out of his sight, but I got a free guided tour out of it! He led me through the whole church, into the Sacresty, the Refectory, the cloisters, and museum. He even let me take a peek at the leather-working school where young people learn the craft. But more than anything else, he told me about the great flood of 1966. On November 4 that year, Florence was completely submerged by the rushing waters of the Arno. And inside this very church, the level reached over 18 feet, as everything from dirty water, mud, and trash rushed in.
Brother Gregorio pulled out an old film, telling me he'd been a witness to the mega flood. The documentary was in black and white - made by a number of cinematographers and produced by famous Florentine director Franco Zeffirelli. It's narrated by Richard Burton, one of the greatest actors during the '60s. The film, says Brother Gregorio, was seen all over the world and gave everyone a chance to see what had happened to Florence. Here are a few frames I was able to catch from the documentary (1-6).

1

2

4

5

6

The *Crucifixion* by Cimabue was one of the most heavily damaged pieces of art. Here are a couple of pictures - before (7) and after (8) the restoration.

7

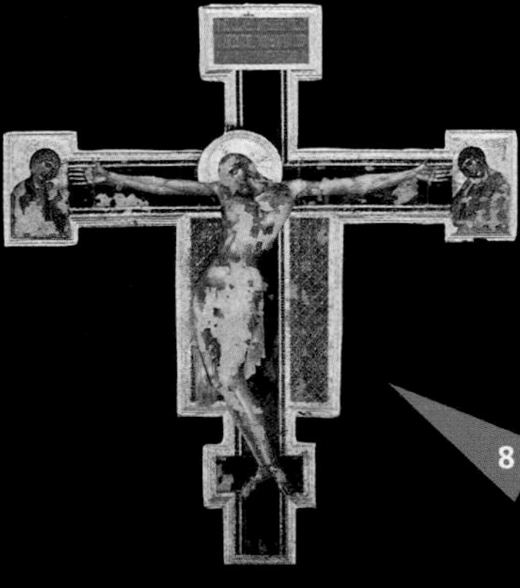

8

1

As you face the church you'll see two very elegant cloisters to your right. The first, dating back to the 14th-century , butts up against the high stone walls of the Basilica and runs the length of one side of the convent, ending in an arcade with a "loggia" (arched balcony) overhead. At the back of the cloister, you can visit the **Chapel** (1) designed by Brunelleschi for the Pazzi family. It's a harmonious and geometric little construction. Proceeded by a portico lined with columns, the chapel is shaped like a rectangle and topped with a cylindrical dome and conical roof. The **exterior** (2) is decorated with cherub heads sculpted by Desiderio da Settignano. The inlaid doors are the work of Giuliano da Maiano. The delightful roundels of **painted ceramic** (3) that you see inside and outside the chapel are by none other than Luca della Robbia. You enter the S. Croce Museum through the first cloister. Fragments of the beautiful frescoes once housed in the church are on display. So are sculptures, stained-glass-windows, and the renowned *Crucifixion* by Cimabue – which has been restored following the terrible damage of the 1966 flood. The **second cloister** (4) (or "Chiostro Grande") was erected in the 15th-century. It's more spacious, enclosed by gracious "pietra serena" columns and dotted with a well in the middle.

3

4

Bargello

5

The Palazzo del Podestà, the "**Bargello**" (5), was built in 1255 to host the "Captain of the People." This was a noble citizen – among the city's bravest – who was charged with watching out for the Republic's security. A few years later, it became the home of the Podestà (out-of-town governor of Florence), then of the Giudici di Rota (an ancient Florentine court) – and finally, the Bargello, also called the Captain of Justice.

This is a massive stone building with narrow little windows, lined with flat-topped crenellations. On one side of the palace a solid square tower rises up like a sentinel. It's nicknamed the "Volognana." At the tippy-top of the tower there's a bell that was once rung to warn citizens of impending danger. The bell – originally located at Montale Castle – is nicknamed the "Montanina." It also rang on other occasions though. Every night, the bell sounded to let people know it was not allowed to walk around with their weapons. A long, drawn-out bell meant someone was being executed. Prisoners languished in the Bargello's jail for long stretches. Some rooms were used for interrogation and torture. The **courtyard** (6) was used for public hangings and decapitations. In 1780 when Grand Duke Leopoldo abolished the death penalty, locals turned the gallows and other torture devices into a bonfire – in celebration of the victory of civility and humanity.

6

In 1859, after the Grand Duke was exiled, the makeshift Governor of Tuscany decided the Bargello should no longer be a jail – and soon converted the building into a city museum holding a magnificent collection of 15th- and 16th-century sculptures. A number of works were subsequently donated by shippers and collectors, turning the Bargello Museum into the world's most important sculpture museum.

1

There's an entire room dedicated to the 16th-century – including Michelangelo's ***Bacco ebbro*** (Drunken Bacchus) (1), the artist's first large-scale sculpture. Another is dedicated to the 15th-century – with Donatello's splendid bronze ***David*** (2). And there's yet another, featuring Verrocchio and his period, where you'll find his lovely ***Donna dal Mazzolino*** (Lady with a Nosegay) (3).

2

Don't miss the magnificent Hall of Arms on the first floor – with breastplates, helmets, and suits of armor – dating from the Middle Ages through the 17th-century. Down in the courtyard you can see the enormous **St. Paul Cannon** (4), named for the big head of the saint found on the barrel.

3

4

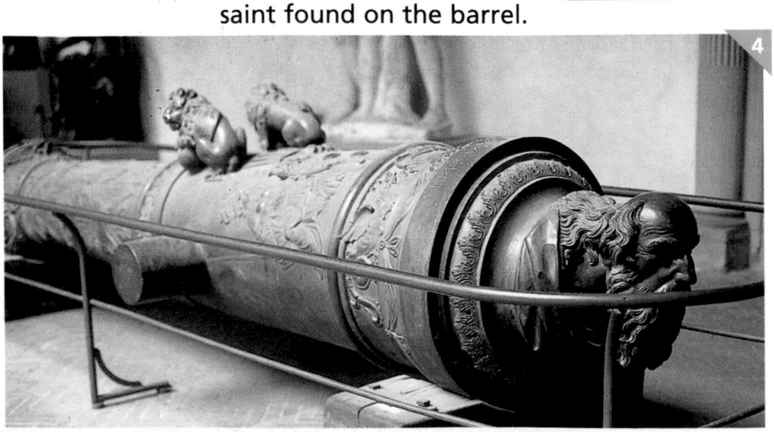

Badia Fiorentina

This is one of the oldest churches in Florence, founded in 928 by Willa, mother of Marquis Ugo di Toscana. It would later be modified a number of times. The first of these was an expansion by Arnolfo di Cambio in 1282; the second, by Matteo Segaloni in 1627. Segaloni decided to move the whole façade – as a matter of fact by "rotating the church by 90 degree's." There's a slim, hexagonal **tower** (5) that lightly reaches skyward to a long point.
Inside the church there are some frescoes from the 13th- and 14th-centuries, a lovely painting by Filippino Lippi, and also, the monument to Ugo di Toscana sculpted by Mino da Fiesole at the end of the 15th-century.
If you follow an out-of-the-way corridor to the right of the apse, you will be treated to a graceful little cloister called the "Chiostro degli Aranci" – named after the orange trees once standing in the flower bed.

5

In the footsteps of Dante...

1

Dante was born in this neighborhood back in 1265, in the Alighieri home somewhere between Torre della Castagna (Tower of the Chestnut – where Florence's old government met before moving to Palazzo Vecchio) and three churches: tiny S. Martino, S. Margherita dei Cerchi, and the Badia. We don't know exactly where the **house** (1) stood. The one you see is only meant as an approximation, a reference point. Dante spent the first years of his life among these narrow little alleyways – overshadowed by the towers of Florence's most prominent families. This is where he met his beloved Beatrice for the first time, where he married Gemma Donati, began his political career, and hung out with his poet buddies. In 1302, however, Dante was exiled and never returned to Florence. Nonetheless, this city remained his greatest and most persistent thought. And in his masterpiece, the *Divine Comedy*, Florence and its citizens are without a doubt the stars.

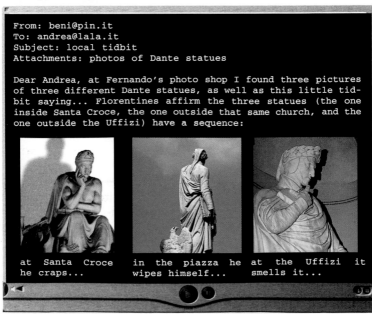

From: beni@pin.it
To: andrea@lala.it
Subject: local tidbit
Attachments: photos of Dante statues

Dear Andrea, at Fernando's photo shop I found three pictures of three different Dante statues, as well as this little tidbit saying... Florentines affirm the three statues (the one inside Santa Croce, the one outside that same church, and the one outside the Uffizi) have a sequence:

at Santa Croce he craps...

in the piazza he wipes himself...

at the Uffizi it smells it...

itinerary 5

1. Central Station
2. Piazza S. Maria Novella
3. S. Maria Novella
4. S. Trinita
5. Santi Apostoli
6. Palazzo Strozzi
7. Palazzo Davanzati

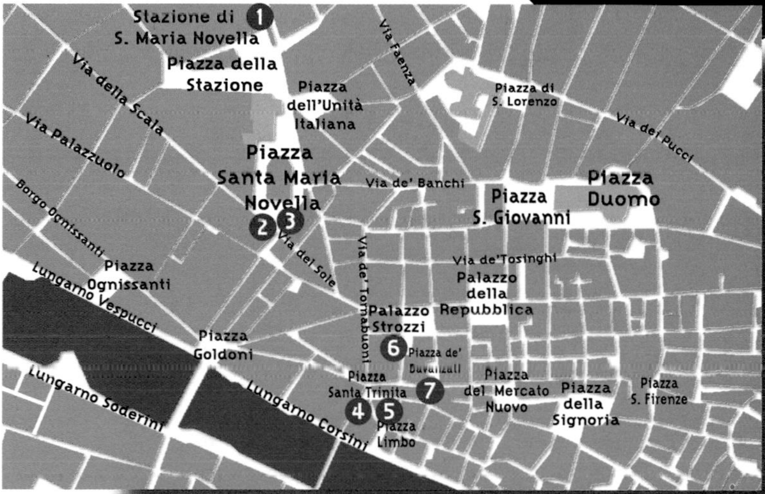

Central Station

S. Maria Novella Station (1) is a beautiful 20th-century construction, built in 1935 by a group of young architects headed by Giovanni Michelucci. The project united the elegance of form to the need for productivity and function. The materials used were mainly "pietra forte" (with its deep yellow color), glass, and iron. The architect Michelucci wanted the station to be comfortable (even people lugging heavy suitcases or having a tough

time getting around can reach the tracks without any obstacles), practical and attractive – even down to the smallest, least important details like the drinking fountains, door handles, benches, lampposts, and platform roofs.

1

Piazza S. Maria Novella

When the Dominican monks arrived in Florence at the beginning of the 13th-century, they chose a little church amid the vineyards outside the city halls: S. Maria delle Vigne. This was the perfect place to start their work. This area was pretty poor, and a lot of the people who worked in the wool factories along the ditches between the Arno and Mugnone lived here.
The Dominican friars – who were called "preachers" for their primary focus on teaching the Gospel to the people – decided their home should first and foremost have a big enough yard to

2

accommodate all the people who came to hear their sermons. So they chopped down the grapevines and built a huge square out front, where the neighborhood locals were more than happy to hang out. But, the monks soon realized that their little church was inadequate for the new crowds they'd attracted. So, being skilled architects as well, the Dominicans started work on a vast new church at the end of the 13th-century. The square was used for sports and festivals from the get-go, not just church business. One of the most famous gatherings to take place here was the "Corsa dei Cocchi." The "cocchi" (light horse-drawn carriages) rounded the square a number of times. They raced between two columns in the shape of elongated pyramids, help up by four stone turtles – specially placed at either end to form a track.

Piazza S. Maria Novella (2) is one of Florence's biggest public spaces – flanked on one side by the lovely church façade and by the elegant 15th-century portico attached to the old St. Paul's Hospital on the other. Beneath the portico's arches, you can see a **lunette** (half-moon) (3) by Andrea della Robbia. This ceramic illustrates the moment when St. Francis and St. Dominic met (the founders of the religious orders of the same name) – right here at this hospital.

3

S. Maria Novella

The construction of this larger church was begun in 1246, under the guidance of two Dominican friars: Brother Sisto and Brother Ristoro. Another friar Jacopo Talenti, designed the magnificent pointed bell tower, completed in 1334. The building took a really long time; the church wasn't officially finished until 1360. All that was left was the façade which was eventually finished in 1470 with

the elegant green and white geometric designs planned by architect Leon Battista Alberti.

Just like S. Croce, Florentines scrambled to be buried here at S. Maria Novella. So, there are luxurious chapels inside. Some people also had tiny family cemeteries in the garden along the church wall. Today, you can see some marble tombs raised atop pointed arches, amid the slender cypress trees. These sepulchers were called "avelli," and the road alongside the cemetery is still called Via degli Avelli.

You'll be stricken at first sight by just how big this church is. Inside you'll see a long nave (300 feet), high ceilings with gothic arches (up to 180 feet), and a little visual trick used by the architects to make the whole place seem even bigger! When they built the columns along the central aisle, they placed them at different distances to create an optical illusion – similar to looking through a telescope. At the beginning, the columns are 45 feet apart, but as you look down, the last sets are only some 35 feet apart.

S. Maria Novella, like all the other churches in Florence, is filled

```
Fr[redacted]peni@pin.it
T[redacted]lickclub@lala.it
Su[redacted]ect: geometry class
Attachments: photo of S. Maria Novella façade with 2nd B class
and Mr. Nello
```

Hey guys, today I ran into a math teacher and his class in front of this church. I heard him say, "Kids, this façade is a masterpiece of Renaissance art. Not only is it a concrete expression of Humanist philosophy; it's also a geometry theorem!" Quite a mouthfu[redacted]huh? The 2nd B class looked a little confused (but also in[redacted]gued) as their teacher flailed his arms around while trying t[redacted]xplain the lines and shapes up high and at the bottom of the façade. I moved a little closer, but had no clue what he was talking about. He was spitting out words like «Euclidean geometry… perfect right angles… distinct geometry of squares and circumferences…» At that point, to get a better grasp of what he was talking[redacted]about, I introduced myself, and Mr. Nello Manganelli let me join his group. That way I was able to find out this façade had more to do with it than just math and geometry: it was also part o[redacted]a scientific study. As a matter of fact at the end of the 16th century, an astronomer named Egnazio Danti put two scientific instruments on it. He put an equatorial "armillary sphere" on the lef[redacted]– made of two rings that represented the meridians, tropics, and[redacted]o on that form a sphere. Depending on the shadow cast on the

with art. Walking down the left nave, one of the works to see is the ***Trinità*** (Trinity) (1) fresco painted by Masaccio in the 15th-century (between the second and third columns). The three divine images are tucked under an arch and vaulted ceiling with arches. These three are God the Father, behind the crucified Son, with the Holy Spirit between them in the form of a dove. To the sides of the painting, you see Mary and St. John. The two noblemen who commissioned Masaccio to paint this work (the "committenti") kneel toward the base. At the very bottom, a reclined skeleton and a macabre inscription remind the visitor of his inevitable death.
In the chapel to the left of the main

1

wall, the armilla would show the different phases of the Earth's rotation. On the right, there's a "gnomon", a complex sun clock where the position and movement of stars could be read depending on how the shadows were cast. Mr Manganelli says that: "this branch of astronomy - 'gnomonics' forms the universal geometric fundamentals we use to observe the heavens."

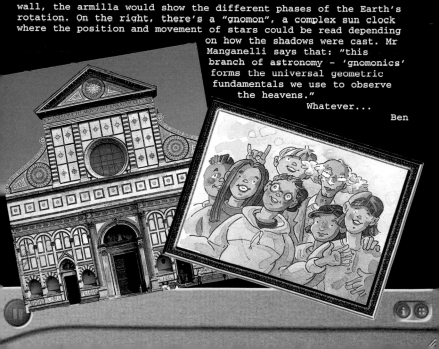

Whatever...

Ben

1

altar, you should go admire the famous ***Crucifixion*** (1) that Brunelleschi sculpted to show Donatello how Jesus should be depicted (if you'll remember, Donatello had also done one over at S. Croce – but Brunelleschi hated it).
Brunelleschi thought Jesus Christ should have a "perfect" face and body, not the coarse ones of a farmer Donatello had shown.
The Cappella Maggiore (Main Chapel) – at the end of the central nave – was frescoed by master 15th-century painter, Domenico Ghirlandaio. ***Stories from the life of Mary*** (2) are painted along the left walls, and of St. John the Baptist and other saints are along the right wall. With the help of his brother, brother-in-law, and possibly even Michelangelo, Ghirlandaio was able to finish these fantastic frescoes, which depict a number of famous artists, writers, and everyday Florentine friends of his – dressed up in their Renaissance clothes.
In the chapel next to this one, another great master decorated the walls: Filippino Lippi. Between 1487 and 1502, he frescoed the chapel for his patron Filippo Strozzi. And as a tribute to his noble financier, Lippi decided to paint the story of St. Filippo in addition to those of other saints.

2

Take a close look at the very interesting scene on the right where ***St. Filippo frees the city of Ierapoli*** (3) from the horrible monster that hid under the Temple of Mars and had killed the King's son with the disgusting smell coming from his body! On the left, you'll see some of the citizens who tried to survive the killer – by plugging their noses!

3

Along the left side of the church, three cloisters open up. The Chiostro Verde (Green Cloister) gets its name from the predominantly green frescoes that cover its walls. These frescoes painted by Paolo Uccello illustrate some scenes from the Bible – including the ***Great Flood*** (4) and the ***Sacrifice of Noah***. The next to come is the Chiostrino dei Morti (little cloister of the dead), a small verdant space full of graves, surrounded by a low arcade. Then, there's the Chiostro Grande (great cloister), completely decorated with 16th-century frescoes. But unfortunately, you can't go there because its' owned by the Military Police Academy today. From the Green Cloister, you can walk into a big space that was called the Sala del Capitolo once upon a time. Later, it was called the **Cappellone degli Spagnoli** (the Grand Spanish Chapel) (5) when Eleonora di Toledo, wife of Grand Duke Cosimo I, designated it for her compatriots' worship in 1540. The "Cappellone" is lined with frescoes by Andrea Bonaiuto, that reflect the Dominican monks' central ethics and tenets. The paintings successfully convey the Order's vision and mission based on the idea that "knowledge conquers all." As a matter of fact, you can see personifications of the arts and sciences toward the bottom: from grammar to music, and from astronomy to geometry and rhetoric.

4

In one of these pictures, you can make out **a pack of black and white hounds** (6) – the colors of these monks' habits. Dominicans called themselves "hounds of the Lord."

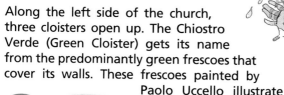

5

6

At the far end of the piazza, over in Via della Scala, you'll find the **Old Pharmacy** (1) run by the friars. Even today, you can still buy perfumes, herbal teas, "miraculous" creams and many types of medicines – all made from the antique recipes of the Dominicans' herbalist shop. The frescoed walls, painted terracotta jars, pestles, distilling devices, and other pharmaceutical paraphernalia are really worth a visit.

S. Trinita

Via Tornabuoni is one of the most elegant streets in all of Florence – famous all over the world for its haute couture boutiques. Walking along the Arno, you'll reach Piazza S. Trinita. At the center is the Column of Justice. The gorgeous Palazzo Bartolini Salimbeni stands to the left, built at the beginning of the 16th-century. In the distance you see the bridge called Ponte S. Trinita, decorated with **statues depicting the four seasons** (2). But the most important building in the sqaure is the **Church of S. Trinita** (3). It was built around 1077 on the site of an ancient oratory (prayer chapel) belonging to the Vallombrosan monks, led by brother Giovanni Gualberto. The friars returned to Florence in 1068, after they had been told to retreat into the Vallombrosa woods by their leader after he'd publicly denounced Bishop Atto as corrupt. After this ordeal, in fact, a monk named Pietro Igneo was able to prove the corruption accusations were valid against, not only Bishop Atto, but also against the new Bishop Pietro Mezzabarba. In 1250 the church and nearby pilgrim hospice were altered (into the version we see today). The façade, however, was redesigned by architect Bernardo Buontalenti at the end of the 16th-century. But it's easy to get an idea of what the old façade

looked like. All you have to do is walk inside the church – and turn around (with your back to the altar). Now, you'll see a simple stone structure with a wheel window and a blind gallery. The interior of S. Trinita is quite dark, so if you want to see the prettiest chapels, you'll need a coin to turn on a light. Don't miss the Bartolini Salimbeni Chapel – the fourth on the right nave. It's enclosed by a fine wrought-iron gate and entirely covered with frescoes of the Virgin Mary and the saints, painted by Lorenzo Monaco. But the real masterpiece is hidden back in the Sassetti Chapel (the second one to the right of the altar). The Sassetti walls are all covered with paintings by Ghirlandaio. In the middle (behind the altar) – you'll see the most intriguing piece: when ***St. Francis brings a child back to life*** (4) after he's just fallen out of a window. In the foreground, you see the child sitting on a large chest – surrounded by his relatives, neighbors, and a group of Franciscan monks. In the background, you see the moment right before: exactly when the young boy tumbles from a window at Palazzo Spini. The scene is painted with such detail and accuracy that you can easily make out Palazzo Spini on the left, the Church of S. Trinita on the right, and the bridge and homes of the left bank (Oltrarno) off in the horizon.

3

4

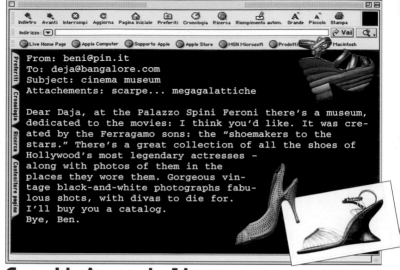

From: beni@pin.it
To: deja@bangalore.com
Subject: cinema museum
Attachements: scarpe... megagalattiche

Dear Daja, at the Palazzo Spini Feroni there's a museum, dedicated to the movies: I think you'd like. It was created by the Ferragamo sons: the "shoemakers to the stars." There's a great collection of all the shoes of Hollywood's most legendary actresses – along with photos of them in the places they wore them. Gorgeous vintage black-and-white photographs fabulous shots, with divas to die for.
I'll buy you a catalog.
Bye, Ben.

Santi Apostoli

Legend has it that **Charlemagne** (1) himself built the church of Santi Apostoli in 805. After being sacked by Totila, king of the Ostrogoths, Florence found its most loyal and powerful ally in the Emperor Charlemagne. The church was erected outside the city walls on the vast, level area near the Arno where unbaptized dead children were buried. That's why the tiny square where the cemetery would have been is called Piazza del Limbo (Limbo Square). Florentine nobleman Pazzino dei Pazzi (whose name means literally the little crazy man of the crazy family) was rewarded some of the stones from Christ's Holy sepulcher. Once he'd come back to Florence, he placed the relics in the church of Santi Apostoli – which were preserved in an elaborate silver and gilded copper container. Every Easter Sunday, these stones are used to strike the fire that will make a carriage blow up in front of the Duomo: the Florentine tradition of "lo scoppio del carro." This is a very old festival, with roots back in the 12th-century – where the pinwheels and fireworks decorating a grand carriage called the "Brindellone" are lit, and the whole thing explodes right there between the Cathedral and Baptistery. This ceremony is said to bring farmers good luck for the upcoming harvest.

1

Palazzo Strozzi

The Strozzi family of bankers, some of the wealthiest Florentines, had an elaborate **Palace** (2) built for them by Benedetto da Maiano at the end of the 15th-century. The massive elegant building was supposed to give the Medici (with their new palace in Via Larga) a run for their money. The palace has a "bugnato" surface of bulging rough stones – which have iron ring hooks bolted into them. These rings were used for tying up horses. On the upper levels, you can see the spiked holders used for placing flags or torches at night to light up the palace.

Palazzo Davanzati

This **Palace** (3) was erected in the 14th-century by the Davizzi family, who had grown extremely wealthy trading British and French textiles. After that the palace passed on to other rich and illustrious merchants – the Davanzati family. Right after they purchased the building, they placed their enormous coat-of-arms on the façade. The tall, narrow palace is supported by a loggia – or arcade – opening onto the street. This is a strange sight because these loggias or "altane" (roof terraces) were used primarily by women and usually opened onto a private courtyard. Decorated with everyday household goods and furnishings, the Palazzo Davanzati now hosts the Museum of the Old-Fashioned Florentine Home. As you stumble through the vast rooms, you get a good

1

picture of how nobles (especially women) lived during the Renaissance. In the large entertaining **halls** (1), you will see dining tables, chests, and credenzas. In the **kitchens** (2): run-of-the-mill appliances and some rare specimens, like the mechanical sifter with a crank, rotisserie, bread kneader, juicers and polenta stirrer. In the **bedrooms** (3): canapies, cradles, rugs. Make a special point to visit the bathrooms or "comfort rooms" – complete with wash basins, hip baths, water pitchers and "showers." Some of the odd things you'll see in some rooms (like the kitchen, dining room and bathroom) are the drawings and scribbles all over the walls. There are proverbs, songs, and notes of daily events. One of the more memorable of these was left in the dining room on the October 6, 1494 by a certain Masino: when a young man was beaten up by thugs. In the kitchen, someone marked the day Giuliano de' Medici was killed. And up on the chimney of a small room on the first floor, someone carved his (or her) romantic longings.

3

2

itinerary 6

1. Palazzo Pitti
2. Giardino di Boboli
3. S. Spirito
4. Carmine
5. Museo della Specola

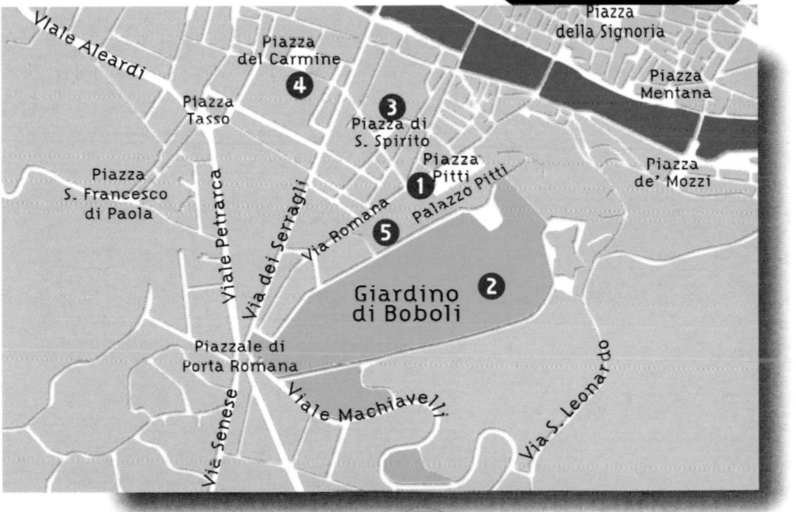

Palazzo Pitti

Luca Pitti was a very rich banker and a great friend and supporter of Cosimo dei Medici (Cosimo the Elder). In 1457 Luca became the "first citizen" of Florence after Cosimo – and the two collaborated to rewrite the Constitution in 1458. It was in this year – at the height of his wealth and power – that Luca decided to build himself a palace. He selected Brunelleschi's designs for the construction (quite possibly the same blueprints the Medici had dismissed as too "over-the-top" for their Via Larga home) and started work up on the Boboli hill.

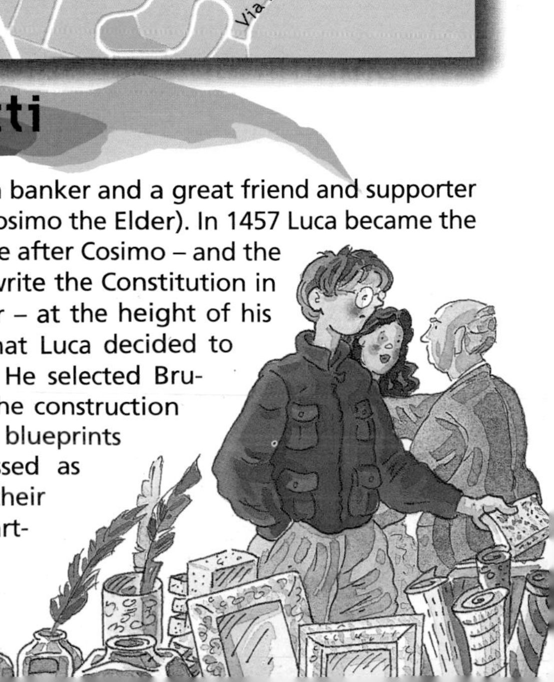

The building was three-stories high, with massive windows, a balcony and an open arcade (loggia) in the center. The entire palace is covered in "pietra forte" (amber-hued). When Cosimo died, two noble Florentines stepped up and took advantage of Luca's aspirations for glory. They promised him he'd become "Lord of the city" if he betrayed Cosimo's son Piero. Piero was able to thwart the betrayal and attracted Luca back to his camp. But it was already too late for Luca, now considered a disgrace by the victors and the vanquished alike. No longer having any credit, Luca had to stop the work on his far-too ambitious palace.
In 1549 Eleonora di Toledo, the wife of Cosimo I, bought the home – and deeming it too "humble" – had Bartolomeo Ammannati expand it. The architect proceeded to build a **marvelous courtyard** (1) near the garden. But the Medici family was still convinced the palace was too small! In 1620 they ordered yet another expansion – this time under the direction of Giulio Parigi and his son. When the Lorena family replaced the Medicis, they also wanted to renovate the palace. They had two wings added on – with terraces and porticoes protruding over the square below. After so many additions, the **Pitti Palace** (2) became enormous; its façade is 615 feet long and 108 feet right in the middle.

1

2

The whole building takes up more than 286,000 square feet. From its beginnings as a private residence, the Pitti Palace went on to become the royal palace of the Medicis, then the Lorenas – and after Italy was unified as a

3

Kingdom – of the Savoia family. Inside the palace, there are a number of different museums: the Palatine Gallery, the Modern Art Gallery, the Silver Museum, Costume Museum, Porcelain Museum, and the Carriage Museum. And of course there are the Royal Apartments, where the Grand Dukes and Duchesses, Kings and Queens lived. You can visit all sorts of Rooms in all sorts of colors: Green, Blue, Yellow and **White** (3) (the grandest of all), and the Ballroom with its crystal chandeliers (where 408 candles once shone against the ceiling – and 540 others glittered against the mirrors along the walls – for a grand total of 948 candles!). Then, there are also the bedrooms, offices, living rooms, and the throne room, where a red throne is covered by an elaborate canopy.

The "Galleria Palatina" (on the first floor) is the oldest and most important of the museums here in the Pitti Palace. This is where you'll find the Medici family's private art collection gracing the palace's elegant halls. Grand Duke Cosimo I had these halls frescoed in 1620 when he started his collection. He chose scenes from classical mythology to give the galleries a more sumptuous and high-brow atmosphere. Among the most notable pieces are: the ***Madonna della Seggiola*** (Our Lady of the Chair) (4) and *La Velata* (the Veiled Woman) by Raphael, ***La Bella*** (the Beautiful Woman) (5) e il *Concerto* (the Con-

4

5

cert) by Titian, as well as numerous family portraits by court painter Giusto Sustermans.
The Modern Art Gallery (on the second floor) showcases works by mostly Italian painters and sculptors from the nineteenth and twentieth centuries. One of the most interesting collections here is

1

the one dedicated to the "Macchiaioli": a group of artists from the end of the nineteenth century who revolutionized traditional Tuscan painting. Their name comes from the word "macchia" – a blot – precisely because they'd apply blots of color to a canvas with wooden pins. They didn't blend these dabs of color. Rather, they left the contrast distinct. Some of the greatest examples of Macchiaioli paintings are by: Giovanni Fattori (*Lo Staffato* – man in stirrups, and the ***Rotonda del Palmieri*** – Palmieri rotunda (1)); Silvestro Lega (*Visita alla balia* – Visit to the Nursemaid); and by Telemaco Signorini (*Veduta di Riomaggiore* – View over Riomaggiore).
The Silver Museum (ground floor) displays exceptional masterpieces of gold- and silver-smithing, enamel, crystal, ivory, and semi-precious stones from the Medici collections. In the Porcelain Museum (over by the Boboli Gardens in the "Casino del Cavaliere") you can see the Medici and Lorena collection of vases, plates, platters and figurines from China and Japan. Or you can admire their porcelain, ceramic and bisque pieces made by the finest Italian, French, Austian, German and English manufacturers (primarily from the eighteenth century). In the Carriage Museum (in the "Rondò delle Carrozze" on the ground floor of the palace's right wing), there are elegant carriages to see from the sixteenth, seventeenth, and eighteenth centuries.
Lastly, you can experience a very unique museum up on the second floor: the **Costume Museum** (2). Magnificent clothing from the seventeenth century up through recent years is on display. These clothes – in mint condition – give you a good glimpse of how closely related our culture is to what we wear.

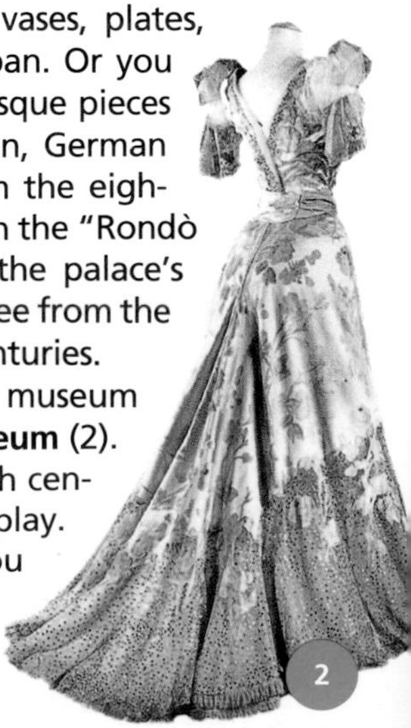

2

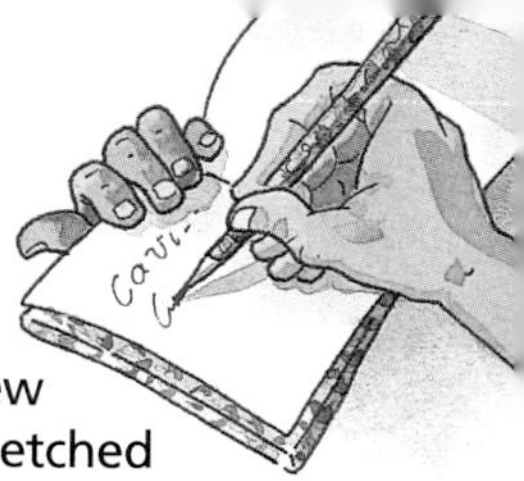

Giardino di Boboli

When Grand Duchess Eleonora di Toledo purchased the Pitti Palace, she also became the new owner of an enormous sprawling "yard" that stretched from the Boboli hill all the way up to the Porta S. Giorgio (St. George's Gate) and back down to the Porta Romana (Roman Gate), along the 14th-century walls. Eleonora transformed these woods and vegetable patches into refined gardens worthy of the newly christened royal palace. A specialist in landscape architecture was chosen for the job: Niccolò Pericoli, nicknamed "Il Tribolo." He transformed the rambling farmland into a well-ordered garden lined with avenues and divided by hedges and orchards with fountains and statues. Right after he finished his blueprints, il Tribolo died. But work on his dream garden continued, with the help of a series of different architects. It was Ammanati – having just finished the final additions to the royal palace – who had the idea of making the garden itself an extension of the Medici's home. He extended the courtyard wings out to the upside-down "U" of the **amphitheater** (3), which Tribolo had designated for performances and sporting events.
The Grand Duke's royal court was always planning elaborate parties and other types of entertainment. In fact, the courtyard itself was often flooded over to stage the "Naumachia" show where ships would engage in live combat. Sometimes, they would put

3

elaborate and imaginative sets up in the amphitheater – a little fantasy park. One of the most popular architects around for these bizarre theatrical specialties was Bernardo Buontalenti. He was nicknamed "Pinwheels Bernardo" for his talent at designing carousels, live performances, masquerades, banquets, and shows featuring spectacular mechanical devices and fireworks. The garden was also used for hunting with traps. Tightly woven rope nets (called "ragne" since they looked like spiderwebs) were thrown on hedges and placed throughout the orchards. A hunting "beater" would scare the birds, until they scattered and hid in the bushes and trees. The birds would get caught up in the snares, and within seconds the game-bags were brimming with blackbirds, thrushes, jays and finches. Besides these festive hunts and parties, guests of the Grand Duke enjoyed special games outdoors – especially walking through the labyrinths. They were so popular that Cosimo II had 3 of these garden mazes built near Porta Romana. The Grand Duke also loved to experiment with cultivating exotic plants in the gardens. Their greenhouse produced dwarf plants, citrus, fruits, and new species of roses, camelias, and peonies (created by grafting and creating hybrids). Evergreen trees (ilex, laurel, cypress, Lebanon cedars, myrtle, and boxwood) provided most of the green throughout the garden. But a number of maple, gingko, and sycamore trees also line the paths and gave the garden splashes of bright fall color here and there.

1

Start your visit to the Boboli Gardens in Ammannati's courtyard, and then walk up to the **Fontana del Carciofo** (1) (the Artichoke Fountain). From here cross the large amphitheater, and take a look at the Egyptian obelisk in the middle. The hieroglyphics on the monument tell its history: it was raised by Pharaoh Sesostri III for the God Ammone around 1850 BC. After you've crossed the amphitheater, walk up the ramps

until you reach a wide pool with Neptune, God of the Sea, in the middle brandishing his threatening trident. This is known as the Fontana del Forcone ("Pitchfork" Fountain).
Turning to your left, you'll walk-past ilex orchards and boxwood hedges... and then you'll see a funny red and white building topped with a copper dome. This is the **Kaffeehaus** (2) (the German-named coffee shop Grand Duke Pietro Leopoldo had built between 1774 and 1775). If however, you keep walking up the ramps over by the Fontana del Forcone – you'll stumble upon a large statue of Abundance, holding up a sheaf of golden wheat in one hand, and a cornucopia of fruit and flowers in the other – symbols of riches and prosperity. Behind this sculpture, you can see the 16th-century walls that enclose the garden. If you follow them to the right, you'll reach the **Giardino del Cavaliere** (3) (Knight's Garden). This is a "secret garden" which you can get to by climbing a flight of stairs and crossing through a tiny gateway. It is completely surrounded by a wall and built on the "knight's rampart" jutting past the garden's edge. In the middle of the garden, you will find the monkey fountain. On one side you'll see the little house built to protect very rare flowers and medicinal plants during the cold winter months. Later on, this would become Gian Gastone dei Medici's favorite spot to study his French. Exiting the gate, walk down the avenue lined with the gardeners' houses, until you reach a clearing called the "Prato dell'uccellare" (Bird-catching Meadow). Turn left and you'll enter the "**Viottolone**" (4) a long downhill road, lined with statues and pointy cypress trees. About halfway down – you'll see the "Cerchiata": a green tunnel formed by intertwined ilex

1

trees. If it's hot outside, the cool shade of the "Cerchiata" will come as a welcome refuge from the sun. Heading to the left, you'll see the walls again – as well as the fantastic **Mostaccini Fountain** (1). Stone monsters with big moustaches (mostaccini) spit water into pools that flow downhill along the path. This was a popular spot for birds to quench their thirst, but back in the days of the Grand Dukes, these pools were covered in "ragnaie" snares. Lots of poor little animals and birds would get caught up in the the nets. If you keep walking along the "Viottolone" path, you'll reach a little space where you can see two statues that depict old-fashioned games. On one side, there's the game of "Pentolaccia." This was kind of like hitting the piñata nowadays. You'd also be blindfolded, but back then you'd use a bat to hit at a clay pot (not a paper-mâché toy) until you broke it, and all the goodies spilled out. The other was called "Saccomazzone," where kids would run around blindfolded trying to strike each other with knotted-up rags. The "Viottolone" ends in the beautiful Pool with the Island a big oval pond full of water games. In the middle there's an island covered in plants and flowers, with the big 16th-century **Ocean Fountain** (2) by Giambologna in the center. The colossal ocean statue rises up from a pedestal, surrounded by the reclining figur-

2

res of three rivers: the Nile, the Ganges, and the Euphrates. You can walk over to the island via two small gated trenches. Statues of Perseus and Andromeda peak out from the water around the fountain. Continuing down the path you reach the Porta Romana after crossing the "Meadow of Columns." But if you'd rather go back toward the Pitti Palace, take the path to the right of the pond, which runs along Via Romana. That way, you'll get a glimpse of the beautiful 18th-century "lemon house" used to store lemon and orange trees during the winter. There are about 500 of these citrus trees today – used back then as well to decorate the gardens. After you walk past the Piazzale della Meridiana (Sundial Square) and the Amphitheater, descend the path toward **Buontalenti's Big Grotto** (3). Grottoes elaborate, fantasy caves were very common sites at the gardens of royal palaces. Buontalenti let his imagination run wild with the grottoes here – and let his passion for set-designing loose. Passing through the wide archway hung with artificial stalactites, you'll enter a space with "spongy" rock walls . (Water used to trickle continuously down the walls – creating a cool lighting effect.) The second setting of the grotto is lined with shells and frescoes and has a statue of Paris and Helen of Troy in the center. The third scene showcases a fountain with a towering statue of Venus.

4

Before you exit, take a quick look at the court jester – **a dwarf called Morgante** (4) – immortalized here, riding a turtle through the pond.

From: beni@lala.it
To: chiara@lala.it
Subject: an evening of dance
Attachments: pictures of Béjart ballets

Chiara did you know that your ballet idol Maurice Béjart also performed here at the Boboli Gardens? I found a book with all sorts of photographs - quite a find. A few pictures are of a ballet from the '70s (have you heard of it?) which must have been really amazing. It was called: "In sweet remembrance of that day" and was inspired by a group of Petrarch's poems. I'm sending you the pictures and technical details.

"In sweet remembrance of that day" (loosely adapted from Francesco Petrarch's "Triumphs")

Choreography: Maurice Béjart

Music: Luciano Berio

Ballet company: Ballet du XXe siècle (20th-century ballet)

Costumes and Sets: Roger Bernard and Joëlle Roustand

Maggio Musicale Fiorentino
Boboli gardens, July 9, 1974

PS: Béjart's last show at the Boboli gardens was in 1997. Versace designed the dancers' costumes.

S. Spirito

The **Church of S. Spirito** (the Holy Spirit) **(1)** gets its name from one of the four original neighborhoods of Florence. It was founded at the end of the 13th-century by a group of Augustinian monks who wanted to create a space for preaching, festivals, and games out front – just like the city's other friars. The church was expanded a century later. In the 15th-century, the famous architecht Filippo Brunelleschi completely redesigned S. Spirito – and topped it with a beautiful dome – covered in terra-cotta scales. He created a symmetrical, balanced interior with no less than 34 columns. The 18th-

century façade is simple, smooth and elegant. There are two cloisters that open off to the right – both from the 16th-century. Toward the back, you see Baccio d'Agnolo's bell tower, dating to 1571. If you go into the church's old convent at no. 29, you can visit the "Cenacolo"(Refectory), frescoed by Andrea Orcagna in the 14th-century.

From: beni@pin.it
To: clickclub@lala.it
Subject: an awesome artist
Attachments: pictures of "animani" and façades

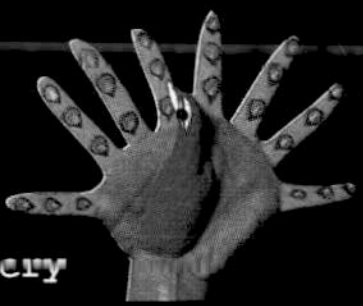

Hey you guys, everyone in this part of town knows all about him. The first person to tell me about him was the clerk at the stationery store, then the artist outside his studio, and finally the florist. And when I went into this place to grab a bite to eat – *boom!*– I saw his work. I'm talking about Mario Mariotti – an artist/inventor who used to live and work in the S. Spirito neighborhood. He was pals with everyone, but had a soft spot for the local artists and craftsmen. He did really weird things: he'd paint his hands and feet to create animals, people, and scenes – you can see all this stuffs in some of the books he made. He used to build totally random objects: a ball that bounced in a strange way ("the crazy dancing ball"), a round book, wooden hats... Hey Mattia – remember the Duomo façades?...well, it's really funny – Mariotti did something just like that here. One night he projected images of paintings by artists from all over the world up on the blank "screen" of S. Spirito's façade. Wow – totally explosive results! All sorts of different, churches and piazzas exploded before people's eyes – in bright, crazy colors.

Ben

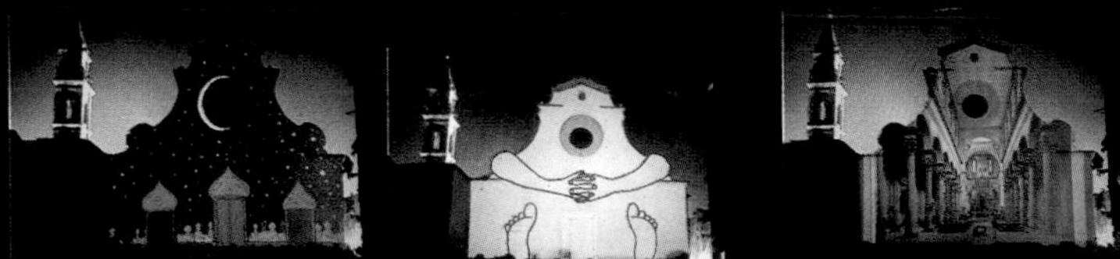

Carmine

1

Building of the Carmine Church started in 1268, but it was only finished once and for all in 1476. However – as was often the case in Florence – the **façade** (1) was never finished. So, even today it looks just like any rustic old wall of rough stone. As a matter of fact, Florentines always preferred to decorate the inside of their churches instead of spending an arm and a leg on marble and exterior carvings. And, in this case, Carmine definitely is home to an exceptional gem! We're especially lucky to be able to see it today given the terrible fire that burned out of control in 1771 and demolished the church. We're talking about the Brancacci Chapel – commissioned by an extremely wealthy and powerful Florentine family (close friends of the Medicis). Between 1423 and 1427 the entire chapel was covered with breathtaking frescoes that illustrated the life of St. Peter. The work was split up between two very talented – and very different – painters. The first was Masolino da Panicale – a refined artist who depicted the world as corteous, ideal, and gentle. The second was a young rebel named Masaccio who painted very realistic notions of the world with his rapid brushstrokes. Once you enter the chapel you'll see the difference right off the bat. In the upper left, Masaccio depicts the moment when ***Adam and Eve are kicked out of the Garden of Eden*** (2). Look at how expressive and dramatic it is. Now look at Masolino's version of ***Earthly Paradise*** (3) up on the right, with the serpent tempting Adam and Eve – painted in an idealized, very

2

3

4

elegant and pleasant fashion. Now, keep on comparing the two artists: up on the left wall, Masaccio depicts a scene from Christ's life (known as ***Il Tributo*** – "the Tax") (4). The portion toward the lower left is particularly stunning, with minimal, powerful strokes. This is the moment when St. Peter opens up a fish's mouth and finds the silver coin he later uses to pay the taxes owed to the priests in the temple (precisely "the tax"). On the wall in front of you, toward the top, Masolino has painted a magnificent Renaissance city with two miracles illustrated on the sides. One is of ***The lame man being healed***; the other is of ***Tabitha being raised from the dead*** (5). The fresco's symmetry and elegance are emphasized in the two refined figures in the center.

When the Medici family lost their power, the family's close allies – the Brancaccis – also fell from grace. So, the monks of the Carmine church decided to erase some of the faces of the many Brancacci family members from the paintings – as they were now considered out of favor and politically "incorrect." But they didn't stop there. They asked Filippino Lippi who later painted the rest of the chapel, to "color over" their erasure marks. It was only in 1989 when the chapel was last restored that many of the "missing" faces miraculously resurfaced.

5

Museo della Specola

In 1775 Grand Duke Pietro Leopoldo unveiled the Imperial Museum of Physics and Natural History in a building along Via Romana. The vast assortment of scientific instruments and specimens collected by the Medicis and Lorenas over the centuries were put on public display. It was the first museum in the world that opened with the following specifications: from 8 until 10 am, commoners could visit ("provided they were dressed neatly," as the rules said). From 10 am on, only well-educated, intelligent people were allowed entrance. Today, this type of distinction seems impossible – but back in the 18th-century, it was considered "revolutionary" to allow admission to everybody. A few years later, the Grand Duke had a tower built so the museum could also have an astronomical and meteorological observatory (to watch the stars and predict weather patterns). That's why the museum was called "la Specola" from that point on – meaning a place to observe the stars. Today the museum boasts a fabulous zoological collection as well. Don't miss the hall of birds (running the gamut from **parrots** (2) of every color to tiny **hummingbirds** (1) and gigantic ostriches), or the hall of Nests, with examples of all sorts of complicated constructions. The "Somalian window" is also pretty fascinating: you'll see a very interesting depiction of the bush in Somalia, complete with the different plants and animals you'd find there. The **anatomical wax models** (3) are also quite cool. This important and well-known collection comes from the "ceroplastics" – or wax modeling – laboratory established here when the museum was founded at the end of the 18th-century. You can check out these models, used for studying the human body – some whole, some in sections focusing on their muscles, internal organs, circulatory system, nervous system, bones. Awesome... but very, very realistic. Kind of creepy...

itinerary 7

1. S. Niccolò
2. The "Ramps"
3. Piazzale Michelangelo
4. S. Miniato
5. Forte di Belvedere
6. Arcetri

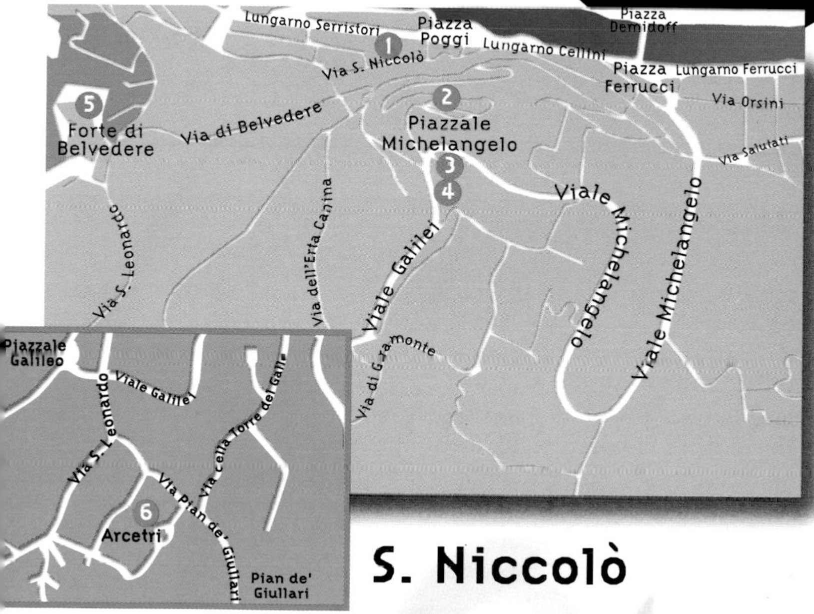

S. Niccolò

S. Niccolò is an old neighborhood in the Oltrarno (Left Bank), nestled between the Arno river and the hills – once home to an extremely poor group of manual laborers. A long time ago, this neighborhood was nicknamed "pidiglioso," referring to the dirty, unhealthy, and lice-infested streets. That was what the area was like until the noble Bardi family erected their homes, palaces, and towers here – in the part of the city where you'll find "Via dei Bardi" today.
At the heart of this neighborhood, you'll see the Church of S. Niccolò sopr'Arno, a small church with a lovely bell tower, dating back to the 12th-century and subsequently modified over the years.

It's said that Michelangelo hid in this very bell tower after an exhausting effort to protect the city with his ingenious fortifications failed – and Emperor Charles V was able to enter Florence.
In front of the church, you'll see the Porta S. Miniato tucked into the walls along the hillside. The massive construction, complete with stairs and buttresses, runs up the **steep path** (1) to the Monte alle Croci.

The "Ramps"

Once Florence became the capital of the young Kingdom of Italy back in 1865, there was a lot of work to do to bring the city up to snuff. Architect Giuseppe Poggi headed one of these projects: to "redesign" the S. Miniato hill. He went on to construct an enormous "balcony" overlooking the city, a broad avenue for carriages to reach it, and a footpath winding through the greenery. This trail is known as "**the Ramps**" (2), and is dotted with fountains and grottoes. The stroll starts down at the Porta S. Niccolò (once a lovely, tall structure nestled into the walls) and rises up for some 150 feet to Piazzale Michelangelo.

From: beni@pin.it
To: brad@sea.com
Subject: some city-planning info
Attachement:

Brad, do you know anything about "urban planning?" I don't really get it, so this info doesn't do much for me. Maybe you'll get more out of it. Back in 1865, an architect named Giuseppe Poggi started up a major renovation project when Florence became capital of the Kingdom of Italy. First off, he knocked down the walls around the city and replaced them with vast avenues, making it easier for horse-drawn buses, carriages, and stagecoaches to cope with the increased traffic to come. Next, he added all sorts of public squares and established two new neighborhoods to meet the needs of a population surge. As a matter of fact, some 30,000 employees of the reigning Piedmontese government moved down here with their families. New bank branches, insurance agencies, and utility companies (most with ties in England) set up shop in Florence. Anyways, with the constant visits form Kings, Queens, and Ambassadors, the city needed to look its best - in step with metropolitan centers like London, Paris, and Vienna. Poggi built a really pretty path through the hills (about 5 miles long), as well as Piazzale Michelangelo, where all the city's visitors came to ooh and aah over the dazzling view of Florence. As a token of their appreciation, the citizens of Florence dedicated a plaque to Poggi here in the square. It says: "Giuseppe Poggi, Florentine architect. Turn around and you see his monument."

Ben

Piazzale Michelangelo

This is a vast balcony looking over the city. At the end of the 19th-century, this monument of Michelangelo was placed in the center of the square. Its statues are copies of the well-known David and the four sculptures adorning the Medici tombs in S. Lorenzo. At the back of the square, you'll notice the "Coffee house" La Loggia – arcade – which was also built by Poggi in hopes of making the tourists' visit all the more relaxing. Behind the Loggia, a cypress-lined stairway leads up to the Franciscan church of S. Salvatore, built at the start of the 16th-century on the foundation of an ancient oratory (prayer chapel). If you're lucky you'll be in Florence between April and May when the gorgeous Iris Garden is in bloom. Beneath the terrace of the Piazzale, you'll see the garden off to the right – where a wide variety of this signature Florentine flower is grows. Piazzale Michelangelo, is without a doubt, one of the best **vista points** in Florence.

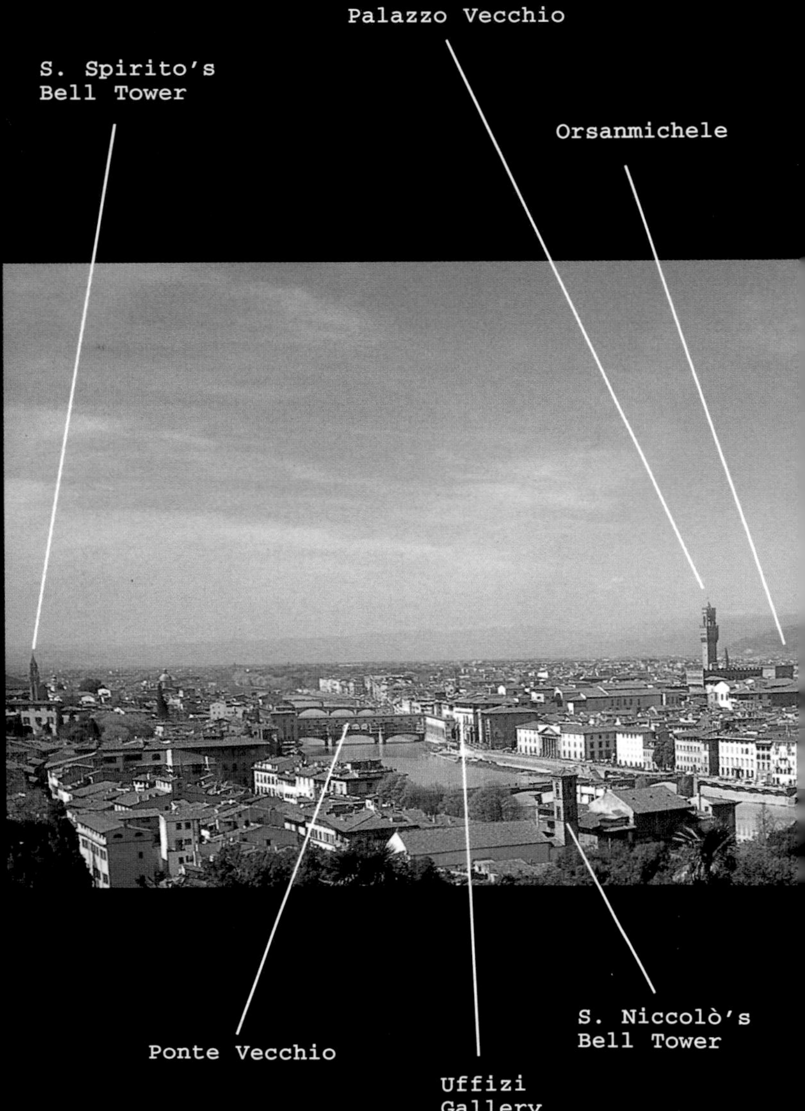
Palazzo Vecchio
S. Spirito's
Bell Tower
Orsanmichele
Ponte Vecchio
Uffizi
Gallery
S. Niccolò's
Bell Tower

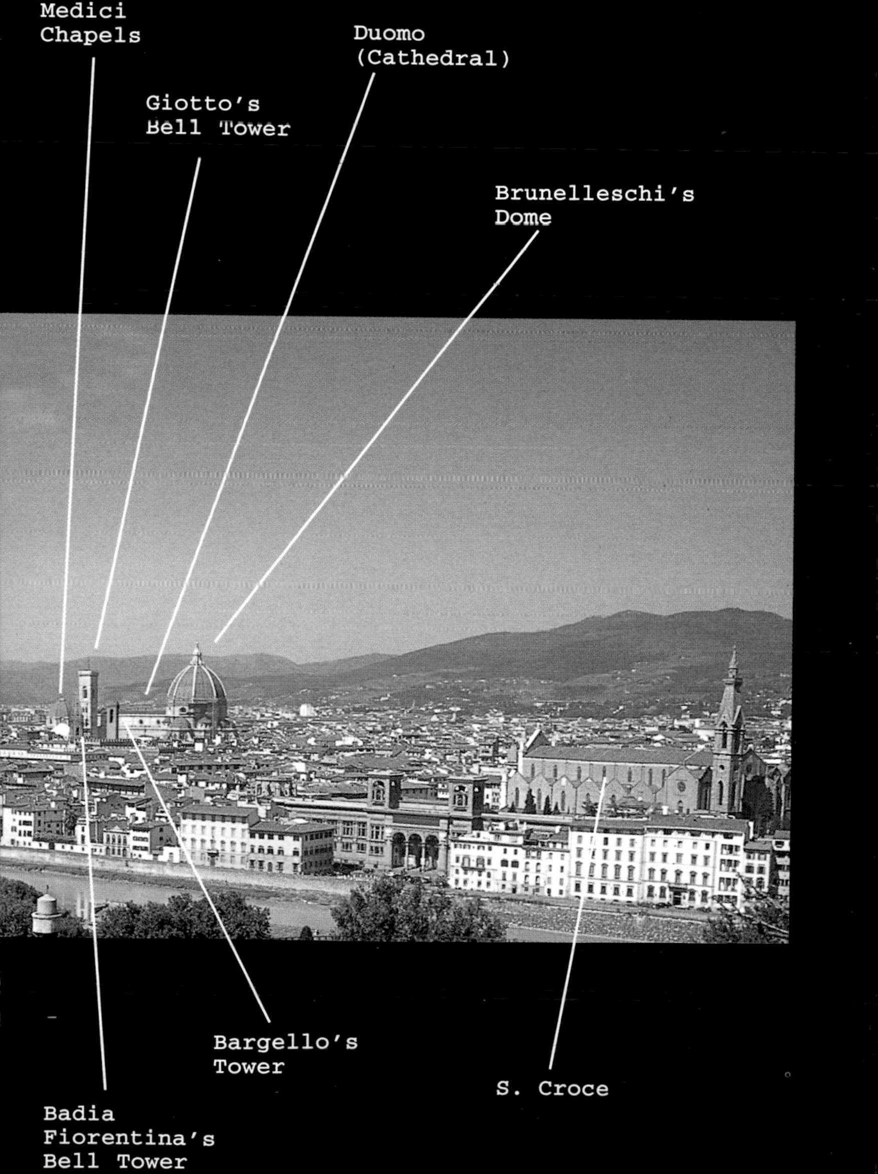
Medici Chapels
Duomo (Cathedral)
Giotto's Bell Tower
Brunelleschi's Dome
Bargello's Tower
S. Croce
Badia Fiorentina's Bell Tower

S. Miniato

A broad stairway leads up from the avenue around Piazzale Michelangelo, known as the Viale dei Colli (Avenue of the Hills). Seemingly out of nowhere, the Church of S. Miniato pops out at you as you climb up to the top of the hill. To the right, you see the Palazzo dei Vescovi (where the Bishops lived in the summertime). To the left, there's a square bell tower made of "pietra forte," surrounded by a very old graveyard called "Porte Sante" (Pearly Gates). S. Miniato was the first Christian martyred here in Florence. He probably hailed from somewhere east of Greece, maybe was even an Armenian King. He belonged to a community of Greco-Oriental merchants, craftsmen, and professionals who'd settled in Florence and brought Christianity with them. The saint's real name was Mynias (where we get the name Miniato), and he was killed in 250 AD during a Christian persecution ordered by the Roman Emperor Decio. According to legend,

From: ben@pin.it
To: clickclub@lala.it
Subject: Akira again
Attachments: pictures of the forts

Hey guys, I just ran into Akira for the gazillionth time - in front of the Church of San Niccolò... Try and guess what he was up to... Yep, you got it! Spending time studying Michelangelo. He dragged me over to the bell tower (and gave the guard a big, fat tip) to see where his idol had hidden out when the Emperor's soldiers were hunting him down. Afterwards, Akira led me up to Piazzale Michelangelo and some of the other «sacred» spots on his "holy pilgrimage." He started to tell me some of the history... It turns out that Emperor Charles V's forces sacked the Republic of Florence in 1529. All of the citizens took up arms to defend themselves - including Michelangelo. He took responsibilty for building up new fortifications. He had a series of ramparts and observation walls built along the hill that ran from the S. Niccolò gate up to the S. Miniato one - protecting both of these churches and the Bishop's palace as well. Artillery squads were stationed up along the defensive bulwarks. When the Emperor started attacking Florence his troops to the South set up camp in the Giramonte hills - directly in front of S. Miniato. So Michelangelo had two cannons positioned atop the bell tower - and from there, shot at the enemies - causing a lot of damage.

the saint escaped unharmed from a number of punishments. He didn't die in a flame-engulfed oven, freed himself from the shackles of the stocks, and was able to make a lion collapse just by making the sign of the cross in the city's arena. When he was at last decapitated, Miniato picked up his head and went to die up on this hill now bearing his name. A chapel was erected on the saint's burial site. In 1018, Bishop Ildebrando ordered a proper church to be raised. It has a beautiful **façade** (1) of green and white geometric marble

But the Emperor's army returned fire – mainly targeting the bell tower. To protect it, Michelangelo tried saving the day with an embankment. This embankment was created from bales of wool and mattresses that wrapped around the base to absorb blows from the stone cannonballs. But the Florentine efforts were in vain. Their own commander Malatesta Baglioni soon betrayed them, and Charles V's troops were then able to topple Florence, bringing the republic to a permanent close. Over and Out! Your war correspondents signing off…

Akira and Ben

2

mosaics – similar to the Baptistery's. At the top, there's a mosaic in the center illustrating Christ on his throne, between the Virgin Mary and St. Miniato. The **interior** (1) is also quite lovely – with three naves divided by columns topped with ancient **capitals** (2). The ground is inlaid with a magnificent array of decorations (whimsical animals, zodiac signs, doves, lions, flowers, and so on). At the end of the central nave, there's a shrine built by the architect Michelozzo upon commission by Piero dei Medici. The shrine is adorned with blue and white ceramics by Luca della Robbia, and has two little painted doors that protect a 13th-century Crucifix. The Cardinal of Portugal's Chapel – off the left nave – is also beautiful. It was erected to accommodate the Archbishop of Lisbon's tomb. This man, Jacopo di Lusitania, died all of a sudden in Florence in 1459. Now go down into the dark **crypt** (3), supported by 36 columns. On the 11th-century altar, you can view the bones of S. Miniato on display. Two staircases rise from the lateral naves – both leading to the top part of the church where the main altar is located – an elegant pulpit on top of a multi-colored marble balustrade. In the apse, you'll see another mosaic from the late 13th-century: this time, an enormous image of Christ blessing between his Mother and S. Miniato. You enter the Sacristy from the right side of the altar. This large square room was frescoed by Spinello Aretino with stories from the life of St. Benedict. Take a close peek at the scene where Benedict is tempted by horrid, **hairy devils** (4)!

1

3

4

Forte di Belvedere

5

In the 16th century, two enormous forts were built in Florence. Both were supposed to defend the city from foreign invaders – but most of all, from the local agitators so feared by the Grand Duke. A low-lying fort called the "Fort of St John" was erected along the city walls (but Florentines have always called this the "Lower Fort"). The other was erected on a hilltop to monitor the enemies' movement, and was called the "Fort on High" or the **Forte di Belvedere** (Fort with a Good View) (5). This spot offers one of the three best panoramas of Florence. Grand Duke Ferdinando I entrusted the fort's design to his brother Giovanni – who got help from the master architect Buontalenti. The fort's foundation is shaped like a six-pointed star – and has four exterior ramparts and two interior ones. A house rises up in the center – meant as a refuge for the Grand Duke's family in the event of a revolt or some other disaster. Buontalenti had this in mind when he built a huge treasure vault with steel-clad doors and built in closets. As a matter of fact, he was also a master of disguise – not to mention great at fireworks and other tricky methods of blowing things up. So he built a cool door, that – when thieves tried to force it open – would shoot and kill them. But he had an even more effective trick ready to protect the family's treasures. He placed a number of water hydrants at the sides of the room. If enemies ever scaled the palace walls, the hydrants would flood the room and make it appear simply like the family's water reservoir. The dungeons are located down in the **tunnels** (6) beneath the palace. One of the most famous prisoners detained here was the pirate Ciriffo, terror of

6

the Tyrrhenian Sea until the Knights of St. Stefano captured him. Ciriffo refused the Grand Duke's proposal of clemency: sparing his life in exchange for converting to Christianity. Instead, he languished away in his dark damp cell until he died.
Today, the Forte di Belvedere is the site of some of the greatest open-air art shows in the world. And visitors get the added treat of one of the most gorgeous views anywhere.

Arcetri

Climbing the hills behind Piazzale Michelangelo, you reach some beautiful spots like the Pian dei Giullari (Field of Minstrels and Jesters) – named after the group of actors and acrobats who used to perform in the halls of a Villa known as "Il Teatro" (the Theater). The small Santa Margherita a Montici church is also up here on a hilltop, as is Arcetri, where you can visit a famous astrophysical observatory. This observatory was built here in 1872 – as an easier place to study the heavens – than the observatory located farther down at the Museo della Specola. Arcetri boasted a cutting-edge instrument: the "solar tower," a vertically fixed telescope used for watching the Sun and stars. This observatory was erected a few feet away from the Villa Il Gioiello (the Jewel Villa) – a gift from Grand Duke Cosimo II to Galileo upon his return to Florence in 1610. The legendary scientist passed the last years of his life up here on the **Arcetri Hill** (1) – working as the Grand Duke's "chief mathematician."

1

itinerary 8

Fiesole

1. Badia Fiesolana
2. Piazza Mino da Fiesole
3. Duomo (Cathedral)
4. Roman amphitheater
5. S. Francesco
6. Scenic tour

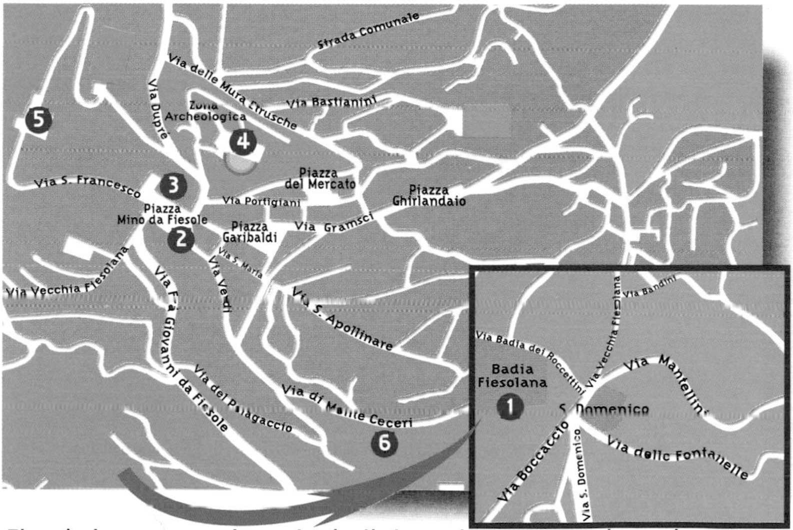

Fiesole is a very ancient city built into the crescent-shaped center of the two-peaked hill looming over Florence. The first inhabitants date back to the Bronze Age. But the city itself was founded by the Etruscans toward the end of the 6th-century BC. The heart of the city was protected by walls that stretched for 7,500 feet and kept the 10,000 residents safe and sound. We know very little about the history of these centuries. We can be certain however, that Fiesole was closely allied with Rome. This relationship allowed the hill town to develop and become quite wealthy up through 225 BC when the Gauls invaded, after descending along the Roman peninsu-

la. When the Romans at last vanquished the Gauls, Fiesole again enjoyed a long stretch of peace and prosperity. That is, until 80 BC when it was reduced to a Roman colony. As a matter of fact, when Silla defeated Marius, he granted a large part of the settlement to his soldiers. This was his way of punishing the people of Fiesole for siding with the enemy. Thus was born the Roman city of "Faesulae," which was one of the region's most vibrant centers.
In the 5th-century Fiesole was conquered first by the Goths, and then by the Byzantines and became poorer and poorer. And so it became impossible for the city to withstand a major decline in status and influence. In fact, Florence, which had emerged in the plains beneath Fiesole's hills, was gaining momentum and becoming very wealthy and powerful. Florence tried to conquer Fiesole a number of times – and finally succeeded in 1125. Even the Bishops – who were established here from 492 AD – abandoned Fiesole and moved to Florence. From that moment on the little hill town was destined to live in Florence's shadow.

Badia Fiesolana

As you climb the hill, you'll come upon the village of S. Domenico about halfway up. There are two gorgeous churches tucked into the countryside. The first is S. Domenico, with its convent and slim bell tower. The other is the **Badia Fiesolana** (Fiesole Abbey) (1), the Cathedral of Fiesole up until 1026. The Badia overlooks the Mugnone valley. It was first built in 1000, but has been revamped a number of times. The last time was 1456, in a project funded by Cosimo the Elder. Surprisingly he didn't commission Michelozzo with the project –. It's very possible that the Badia was designed by Brunelleschi, who gave the plans to Cosimo before he died in 1464. His death brought the construction to a halt and leaving the façade unfinished. Nonetheless it is quite lovely: rough

stone, with the old green and white marble design preserved in the middle. A façade within a façade, you might say.
Today the Badia Fiesolana serves as the European University campus, thrusting this tiny, isolated church into the international spotlight.

Piazza Mino da Fiesole

Piazza Mino da Fiesole is found at the center of the city – on the site of the ancient Roman Forum. Walking into the square from the road where S. Domenico Church is, the first thing you'll see on the left is the large seminary (where young men study to become priests). Then you'll see the Bishop's Palace built in the 11th-century. The Cathedral stands across the street, with its bell tower in the shape of a Medieval turret. At the far end of the square, you can see the Palazzo Pretorio. Its loggia (or portico) covered with coats of arms from the various podestàs (the foreign rulers), the palace is now city hall. Next door is the very, very old little church of St Mary Primerana. In the middle of the square, there's a monument commemorating the 1860 **Meeting at Teano** (2): when Garibaldi shook Victor Emmanuel II's hand and recognized him as the first King of Italy.

Duomo (Cathedral)

The Cathedral of Fiesole is dedicated to the city patron, St. Romulus. It was built between 1024 and 1028, according to Bishop Jacopo il Bavaro's wishes to make the Cathedral more stately than the Badia Fiesolana. It is a large and quite simple edifice,

almost entirely rebuilt in the 19th-century, privy of marble panels and other embellishments – just stone. Within the vast three-naved interior, you will see works by the most significant sculptors from Fiesole. There's a beautiful **bell tower** (1) next to the church – dating back to 1213. The square tower is 130 feet tall with a crown of flat Guelph crenellations.

Roman amphitheater

On the backside of the Fiesole hill, overlooking the Mugnone valley and Apennines' peaks, you'll find a marvelous **Roman amphitheater** (2) excavated amid the rubble. It's in the shape of a semi-circle, with 19 descending rows that could have held some 3,000 spectators. The space is quite large in all, and in the nearby museum, you can check out some of the theater's fragments and decorations. If you descend on the left while exiting the amphitheater, you can make out the ruins of a 2nd-century BC thermal spa, discovered at the end of the 19th-century. There's a large pool that was used for bathing, as well as some others used to filter water. You can still see traces of the boiler room where water was heated, as well as the round furnaces and remains of the three con-

tainers separating cold, warm, and hot water. Along the middle wall, you'll see the big tube which was used for pumping steam into the different rooms.

To the left of the amphitheater are the ruins of a small **Roman temple** (3) from the 1st-century BC – and further down, you'll see the ruins of an Etruscan one from the 3rd-century BC. To the left of this last temple, there are remnants of a door which likely linked to the imposing Etruscan walls (constructed of massive stone blocks piled on top of each other) leading to the Roman baths. In the adjoining Archaeological Museum, you find votive figurines (for worship) bas-reliefs, and many other surprises that will give you a vivid picture of what it would have been like to live in Fiesole during Etruscan, Roman, and Lombard times.

S. Francesco

If you want the most breathtaking view of Florence and the Arno Valley possible, walk from the main piazza up the path leading to the S. Francesco hill. Up here, you find a little church with the same name, on the grounds where the Etruscans had once built an acropolis. Trust us, the view is worth it!

Scenic tour

The hills around Fiesole offer a number of options for hiking and bike and bus rides. One possible route leads from Fiesole's square up to Borgunto, over the hill's ridges on "Bosconi Road," and over to the "Quadrivio dell'Olmo" (Elm Crossraods). From this point, you can choose to follow the road heading for Faenza, for Mt. Senario, for the "Molin del Piano" (Windmill in the Plains), or for Florence via the Mugnone Valley. On a clear day, the panorama is exquisite, with the Tuscan and Emilian Apennines off in the distance. The other option leads off in a different direction from the first itinerary – somewhere around the Baccàno fork in the road – winding through oak, cypress, and ilex trees. Following that route, you'll

arrive at the Castel di Poggio (a massive castle with a lovely, light stone, square tower) – and then at the Castello di Vincigliata (a castle built in 1031 and restored in the 19th-century, with crenellated walls and a looming, high tower).
A variation on this tour is to climb Mt. Ceceri (1245 ft.) by following the paths hidden away behind the thick bushes.
The third itinerary takes you to the famous Maiano Caves – where Florentines excavated their precious "pietra serena." This grayish blue stone was used to construct countless buildings in Florence. To get here, take the road (Via Benedetto da Maiano) halfway up the hill – veering off the "Regresso" (drop-off) curves. Once you arrive at the intersection of three streets, hang a left, and go from Maiano up through the cypress, ilex and birch forest, until you finally reach the cave's stone walls.

From: beni@pin.it
To: chiara@lala.it
Subject: building a mechanical bird
Attachments:

Hi, Chiara! Guess what happened to me today? I was sitting and reading next to a statue in the Piazza di Fiesole, when a tail started wagging between the pages and my lap. It was a brown dachshund named Homer, brushing up against a German tourist and panting at him like they were old pals. I figured out pretty quickly that he was lost, so I did my good deed for the day and decided to bring him home. The address was on his collar: Homer, Villa Il Giaggiolo. After looking everywhere, I finally found the Villa gate, and rang the bell. An old British nun answered the door. Within minutes, she had me drinking tea and listening to a gazillion stories. Here's one that might appeal to your "inner mechanic". Right around the Villa Il Giaggiolo there's a mountain called Mt. Ceceri. This is where Leonardo da Vinci attempted his most daring feat of all: flying. Along with his two young assistants, Zoro and Giacomo, Da Vinci had built this huge mechanical bird, similar to a white falcon: an "astore" hawk. It had two ridged wings lined in silk, that fit into a structure that tapered in a fanned-out tail. There were no levers, gears or metal tie-rods back then. Da Vinci had calculated that the breeze coming from the East would push the huge bird along a trajectory whose angle ended in the fields over by S. Salvi - and that the flying machine would land smoothly due to the perfect proportion between weight and volume. But he hadn't taken the crosswinds into account. So, his prototype was blindsided, started to plummet, and crashed after only getting a few feet up in the air. What a bummer - poor Da Vinci! Later,

Ben

itinerary 9

1. Cascine
2. Giardino degli Orti Oricellari
3. Fortezza da Basso
4. Giardino Stibbert
5. Giardino dell'Orticoltura
6. Villa Demidoff

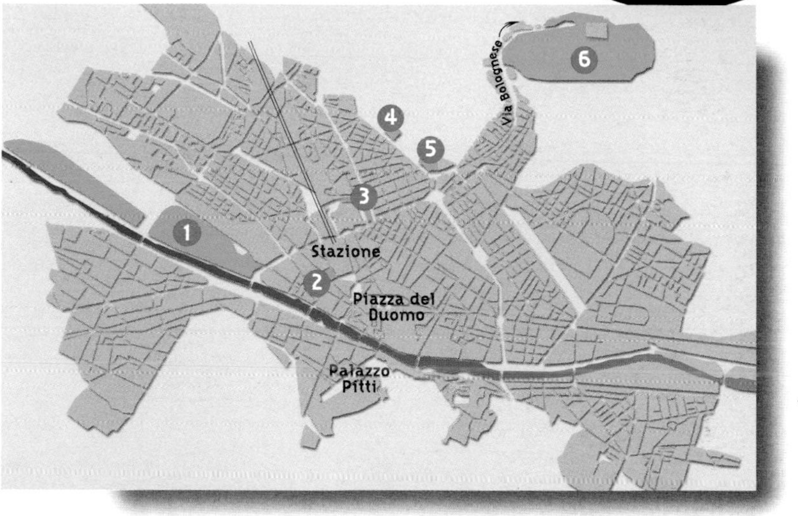

Cascine

The Cascine is the largest park in Florence, 295 acres of level terrain stretching for 2 miles along the right bank of the Arno River, up to the confluence with the Mugnone stream.

Inside the park there's a public swimming pool, two horse-racing tracks, tennis courts, ranges for archery and both target and skeet shooting, the University of Florence's School of Agriculture and Forestry, and the elite Military School for air-combat training.

In the 16th-century the Arno was characterized by a bunch of tiny islands in this area. The one called "Cascine dell'Isola" is more or less where today's park stands. In 1531, Alessandro dei Medici bought this property and transformed into fields for raising cattle. For a long time, the Grand

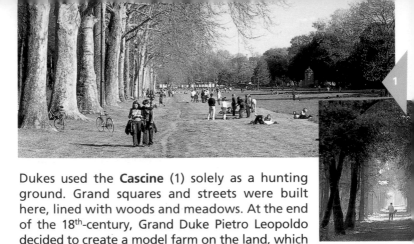

Dukes used the **Cascine** (1) solely as a hunting ground. Grand squares and streets were built here, lined with woods and meadows. At the end of the 18th-century, Grand Duke Pietro Leopoldo decided to create a model farm on the land, which would be open to the public as a living example of his new agrarian policies. He went ahead and commissioned Giovanni Manetti, a young architect who'd recently finished his studies in Rome, for the project. Manetti started to design fanciful gazebos, statues, and piazzas lined with columns; but then the Great Duke decided to step in. He reminded Manetti he was supposed to design a farm, not the Boboli Gardens! So, the architect set about designing a lovely building in the heart of the park, decorating it with

medallions of cows and bulls. He erected large stalls and haylofts, an elegant watering trough in the "Prato del Quercione" (Oak Meadow), a **pyramid** (2) to keep ice frozen during the summer, and two little templets which were used as aviaries for peacocks and pheasants. The park officially opened to the public July 3, 1791 with an enormous bash that went on for three days! From that moment on, Florentines have considered the park one of the best places to play and go for a stroll.

The park spreads out along a central elm-lined avenue, the viale degli Olmi – where you'll also find linden, hackberry, and *Celtis* trees. Tucked amid beautiful lawns and dense woods you can walk through the Prato della Tinaia – surrounded by fragrant lindens and a magnificent **flowering magnolia tree** (3) –, the Prato del Quercione – named after the huge oak that once loomed in the middle, and the half-moon-shaped "Prato delle Cornacchie" (Meadow of Crows). Next to this last meadow, you can see an amphitheater and the "eight paths," a kind of labrynth. At the end of the park where the Mugnone meets the Arno, you'll see the **Monument to the Indian** (4). This pagoda-like temple encloses a statue of Rajaram Cuttraputti, maharajah of Kolapoor. The young prince died in Florence in 1870, and his ashes were thrown into the confluence of the two bodies of water – in keeping with the Brahmin tradition.

```
From: beni@pin.it
To: plato@lala.it
Subject: pretty dogs
Attachments:

My dearest Plato, Here's some news you can share with some
of your girlfriends. It's got to do with pretty dogs (so
don't even consider yourself…). Every year, here at the
Cascine there's a big dog show where the loveliest canines
around - of every breed - strut their stuff. And they're
all combed, polished, and very graceful (unlike you!).
                                                      Ben
```

Giardino degli Orti Oricellari

Near the Porta al Prato, there is a fantastic garden enclosed behind the gates of elegant homes – where you can visit only with the permission of the groundskeeper. We're talking about the Orti Oricellari (at number 48 on the street of the same name). This garden was built in the 15th-century by a group of artists and intellectuals for plays, concerts, and get-togethers. Tucked between the trees, you can see the enormous statue of the giant **Polyphemus** (5) in the center of the garden. Almost 27 feet tall, it was sculpted by one of Giambologna's students, Antonio Novelli.

Fortezza da Basso

In 1535, Alessandro dei Medici commissioned Alessandro da Sangallo to design the Fortezza da Basso (Lower Fort) – also known as St. John's Fort. This imposing building, along with the Forte di Belvedere, was used to defend the city from all enemies – both at home and abroad. It has massive walls made of stone and red brick and four large horizontal ramparts. Up until a few years ago, the fort was still used as a military storage depot. But nowadays, it serves a totally different purpose: as the city's biggest convention center.

Next to the fort, a garden winds along the city's busiest avenue. The park was planned by architect Giuseppe Poggi during an urban renewal project back when Florence was the Kingdom of Italy's capital. In the center, there's a huge **pool** (1) where white swans swim – with a spouting fountain and two tiny rock islands covered in foliage.

Along the little road following the walls, you'll find enormous **cedar trees from Lebanon** (2), the Atlas, and the Himalaya Mountains. But the rarest tree of all is the Eastern "paulonia" (*Paulovnia tomentosa*), named in honor of Anna Paulovna, daughter of Czar Pavel I of Russia.

2

1

Giardino Stibbert

The garden and the villa here belonged to Frederick Stibbert, an eccentric British collector of art from faraway lands – with a thing for historical weapons and armor. The castle-like villa is a fun, but weird, museum. There are rooms filled with suits of armor, medals, halberds (battle axes on spears), and flags of practically every country. Don't miss the Oriental halls (with maharajahs and Indian knights, "Maharani," and foot soldiers), and the Japanese halls (with warriors and archers, Mandarin uniforms, scimitars, and daggers). But the **"Sala della Cavalcata"** (3) is the coolest of all: there's a caravan of 14 knights and infantrymen from the 16th-century – all decked out with original Spanish, Italian, German, and Arab armor and weapons.

The garden is laid out strangely: part of it is flat, while the other part slopes down with little steps and paths. It is chock-full of tall trees, bushes and hedges – with mini lakes, caves, statues, arcades, and **little temples** (4) popping up here and there – giving the place an air of mystery. Besides pines, oaks, cypresses, ilex, and beech trees,

there are a few exotic and rare trees in the garden. At the entrance, there's a **Judas tree** (1), and in the back by the avenue, there's a "calocedrus" with branches like a candelabra, as well as a humongous cedar of Lebanon. Next to the stairs, you see a wild strawberry tree from Greece – called the "skin tree" because its copper-colored bark tends to "peel" easily.

Giardino dell'Orticoltura

This garden was built around 1865 by the Tuscan Horticulture Society (an association that studied techniques for cultivating flowers and plants), and became property of the city in 1930. When you enter, you'll see the **greenhouse** (2) – an elegantly crafted, large glass and cast-iron building. It was constructed in 1880 by architect and botany enthusiast Giacomo Roster, who had the famous British greenhouse, the "Crystal Palace," in mind. It was used to protect delicate and exotic plants from the harsh winter chill. The structure is immense (about 120 feet long, 51 feet wide and 42 feet high), and is surrounded by a portico. The garden has a rich assortment of trees, among them magnolias, planes, oleander, and crepe myrtle. And close to the greenhouse, there's an interesting tulip poplar (*Liriodendron tulipifera*) with its characteristic flowers shaped like – you guessed it – tulips.

Villa Demidoff

Francesco I dei Medici bought this vast Pratolino estate in 1568. With the help of the architect Bernardo Buontalenti, he created what became a mansion of marvels and delights: a sort of Renaissance amusement park. More than anything, Francesco wanted to impress and enchant the gorgeous Venetian woman he loved, Bianca Cappello. As a matter of fact, once the project was finished, she liked it so much that she often retreated here for long spells.

Buontalenti was definitely the right man for the job. He was an expert in all facets of architecture, but was particularly talented when it came to bizarre, fantasy constructions with unexpected theatrical effects. Surrounding the villa – as beautiful and big as a royal palace (complete with secret rooms and mechanical marvels) – were labrynths of laurel trees, and grottoes (including the Caves of the Flood, Tritons, Frogs, the Stove, the Sponge, **Cupid** (3), and the Bear). There were also grand fountains – like the one of the Chickens, the Farmer, the Oak, Perseus, Aeschulapius (god of medicine), and the **Mugnone stream** (4). There were places just for playing, either riding on the merry-go-round or playing old-fashioned ball games called "palla-corda" and "pallottolaio," fish ponds, aviaries, pools, and best of all, water games. A stream was channeled to flow down Mt. Senario, dumping water into a series of pipes. This moving water set off a chain reaction: with water, the mechanical fountains, games, and monuments all started to work. One of the coolest effects could be seen along a 290 yard stretch on Viale degli Zampilli: a series of jets shot up a shower of colored water that arched like a rainbow.

3

4

Francesco's successors didn't care much about the Pratolino villa, and eventually, the

1

whole estate went to ruins. In 1814, Ferdinando III of Lorena decided to transform the garden into an English-style park, and demolished the villa, in terrible shape by then. In the second half of the 19th-century, the property was sold to Prince Paolo Demidoff, who cleaned the place up. He had the gardens spruced up and restored

2

the old villas. And when he was through, he moved into one of them: "La Paggeria."

In recent years, the Villa Demidoff Park became public property so that everyone can visit and enjoy it now. But don't come hoping to see the "garden of marvels" Francesco made for Bianca though. You can, however, catch a glimpse of a few fabulous things here and there. Best of all is Giambologna's gigantic statue of **Apennine** (1), which towers above a little lake. Get this – inside the giant's head, there's a room – and his eyes are the windows! You shouldn't miss the beautiful Fountain of Zeus either, up at the highest point in the park. The mysterious Grotto of Cupid, the **Viale degli Zampilli** (2), and the famous Shrimp Pools – once actually used to raise crustaceans – are also worth a peek.

what are these?

Brief glossary of some of more difficult terms used in this guide

Acropolis: raised, walled portion of Ancient Greek cities – which housed important public and religious buildings.
Altana: terrace covered with a loggia on the roof of a building.
Amber: orange-brown hued resin, mostly used for decoration and jewelry.
Apostles: the 12 disciples of Jesus who spread his Gospel.
Apse: architectural term for the back of a church. It is often a semi-circle behind the altar.
Astronomical Observatory: building equipped with such scientific instruments as telescopes, light meters, and spectroscopes – used for watching and studying the heavenly bodies.
Atlas Cedar: evergreen tree, shaped like a very high pyramid – native to Morocco and Algeria, has grayish foliage.

Balaustrade: parapet formed by columns and pilasters that support a curtain – often used in churches to separate spaces reserved for clergy.
Baptismal font: tub inside a Baptistry or church, filled with holy water used for christenings.
Baptistry: sacred building used for christenings – with a geometric base and a baptismal font inside.
Bas-relief: sculptures, where the figures emerge in 3-D from a wall.
Bastion: structures placed at the corners of forts for re-enforcement, formed of a floor surrounded by protective walls.
Biphora: window divided into two identical openings by a central column.
Bisque: white porcelain used for decorations.
Bugnato: decoration used on the outside walls of Renaissance palaces – made of rough stones jutting from the walls: "bugne."

Calocedrus: large tree from North America – up to 90 feet high, with red bark and candelabra-shaped branches.
Capital: top portion of a column where arches rest. Capitals are categorized by their shape and decoration.The most well known are Doric, Ionic, and Corinthian.

Cedar of Lebanon: evergreen tree, shaped like a very high pyramid – native to Lebanon, has dark-green foliage.

Celtis: tree that grows 45-60 feet high in temperate zones – with rough leaves and blackish berries.

Ceramics: term used to describe a number of objects made from clay, baked in a kiln. Depending on the type of baking (variations in the temperature), and the covering (enamel, glaze, etc.), you can create terracotta, majolica, *grès*, porcelain, etc.

Chest: piece of furniture shaped like a trunk or large box – often decorated, inlaid, or painted – very common in Medieval and Renaissance times for holding clothes, linens, and a bride's trousseau.

Choir: stage within a church where the choir sits.

Cloister: courtyard in the shape of a square or a rectangle, enclosed by porticoes – next to a church or within a convent.

Coral: the lime-based skeleton of an ocean coelenterate which is found along coastlines and rocky reefs. Its color varies from light pink to bright red, used for decorations and jewelry.

Cornucopia: a vase or basket shaped like a ram's horn – full of herbs, flowers, or fruit – an ancient symbol of abundance.

Cotto: *see* Terracotta.

Crenellations: the tooth-like ornaments lining the top of fort walls, or the walls of palaces and towers. The crenellations can either be Guelph (flat-topped rectangles) or Ghibelline (shaped like swallows' tails).

Crypt: underground portion of a church – located beneath the main altar. Historically this was used to house the tombs or relics of saints.

Dome: architectural structure used to cover a building (usually a church) or a portion thereof. The half-sphere top rests on a circular or multi-sided base.

Double lamppost: lamppost that would hold candles, candelabras or torches.

Enamel: a glass-based glaze – in a range of vivid, glossy, or opaque colors – used mainly in jewelrymaking.

Fiancata (Flank): side portion of a church or monument.

Foundry: place where metal and works of art are created by a forge. Using an artist's model (in plaster, resin or wood), a form is made – a hollow mold where forged metal is poured. The rough resulting piece will be rid of extraneous pieces and cleaned up and smoothed by the foundry metallurgist.

Frame: in architecture, the sum of the materials used to support a structure during construction.

Fratina: long, narrow table used in monastery refectories.

Fresco: mural painting technique. The wall is prepared with a thick application of lime and sand. A thin layer of the mixture is then spread on top of this. Then, the outline (sinopia) of the work is drawn, followed by another thin layer of this mortar. The colors are then rapidly applied "a fresco" – that is while the wall is still moist. That way, the colors are absorbed by the mortar and dry together with it.

Frieze: ornamental "sash" or swag decorated with figures or geometric motifs.

Gingko biloba: a plant native to China – with fan-shaped leaves that turn bright yellow in Fall.

Greek "strawberry" tree (*corbezzolo*): evergreen tree commonly found in the Mediterranean brush of Eastern regions. It is characterized by an orange trunk and peeling bark – giving it the nickname "skin tree."

Halberd: ancient weapon shaped like a battle axe with steel blades like spears.

Halo: in sacred art, the shining ring above the heads of saints.

Heretics: those who oppose the teaching of the Church.

Hieroglyphics: a design comprised of stylized figures – typical of Egyptian writing.

Himalayan Cedar: evergreen tree, shaped like a very high pyramid – native to the Himalayas and Afghanistan – has green foliage.

Hip bath: a small bathtub in which you stay seated.

Hospice ("Ospizio"): building used to house pilgrims, orphans, and the sick, handicapped, or elderly once upon a time.

Hydra: mythological serpent monster with 7 heads.

Inlay: a type of work on wood or marble of various colors – created by laying small pieces of wood or marble into various designs – works of art in their own right.

Judas tree: small, ornamental tree, native to Asia Minor (near Turkey today), characterized by its lovely pink blossom in Spring.

Lagerstroemia: ornamental plant with deep pink flowers, native to Australia, Southern Asia and South America.

Lantern: architectural term used to describe a small geometrical structure – placed atop a dome to let light in. On top of the lantern, you'll usually see a ball or a cross.

Lapis lazuli: decorative, deep blue stone used in jewelry, inlay, and other ornamentations.

Liriodendron tulipifera: large tree native to the United States – with yellow tulip-shaped flowers.

Madia: a kitchen cupboard (for storing bread, etc.) used in Tuscany centuries ago

Maharajah: title given to Indian princes or feudal lords.

Maharani: title given to the Maharajah's wife.

Main altar: the principle altar in a church, usually in the center and elevated.

Mandarin: term used in ancient China to describe a member of the elite, a very influential person.

May Day: the first of May. In Florence, this was the festival of Spring – harking back to Medieval times.

Mosaic: artistic composition of tiny glass, stone or ceramic tiles in a gamut of colors – all held together by cement or a type of mortar.

Mother of Pearl: the interior of the shell of some mollusks (like oysters).

Naumachìa: an elaborate production where naval battles are staged in amphitheaters, circuses, or town squares – forcibly flooded with water.

Nave: the central or side aisle of a church, bordered by columns or pilasters.

Obelisk: Egyptian monument measuring between 60-90 feet – formed of a single block of stone, resting on a square base and tapering to a point at the top. It's usually decorated with engravings, hieroglyphics and bas-reliefs – and was placed on the side of a temple entrance in honor of the Pharaoh and his victories.

Onyx: a types of agate, often whitish with darker veins, used for jewelry or decoration.

Oratory: small building set apart or connected to a church or convent – used for communal prayer.

Patina: the exterior sheen or coloring objects acquire with age or exposure to the elements.

Patriarchs: the ancient progenitors of the Jewish people – such as Abraham, Isaac, and Jacob.

Paulonia: a large, ornamental tree measuring 30-45 feet – native to China – with large leaves and pink blossoms.

Pietra forte: a yellowish type of sandy stone used to construct palaces, foundations, and floors.

Pietra serena: a crumbly stone with a light gray hue used to adorn the exteriors and interiors of Florentine buildings.

Plans: a reproduction of a building (or a part) drawn on a horizontal plane – like paper (blueprints for example)

Porcelain: a particular type of ceramic derived from a hodge-podge of minerals. The compact, white "clay" with mother-of-pearl highlights was invented by the Chinese in he 1st-century BC. It's primarily used for plates (or "china"), vases, and figurines.

Prophets: wise men from the Old Testament who received inspiration from God, such as Abraham, Isaac, and Jacob.

Pulpit: a raised "stage" used for preaching – found inside churches. It can be constructed of a wide variety of materials (wood, stone, marble, etc.) and is often intricately decorated with bas-reliefs.

Pumice: very light volcanic stone "spewed" in the air during eruptions – colored light gray.

Ragna: a network of ropes cast over bushes or tree branches to catch birds.

Refectory: a large dining room found in convents, colleges or other places where there is communal living.

Sacristy: the place inside a church which serves as the wardrobe for clerical vestments and other sacred linens, like altar cloths.

Sala del Capitolo: the room where Bishops, priests, or monks gather to deal with the administrative business of a church, cathedral, or convent.

Sarcophagus: an ancient funerary container – or chest – made of stone, marble, alabaster, terracotta or wood.

Scimitar: a type of curved sword used in the Orient.

Selciato: a type of floor made of multi-shaped stone slabs – found on streets or courtyards and town squares.

Self-portrait: portrait of a painter, painted by himself.

Semi-precious stones: very hard minerals or rocks of a variety of colors. Semi-precious stones are frequently used in jewelrymaking.

Stained-glass window: a large wood or metal framework in which multi-colored glass tiles are inserted to depict geometric shapes or scenes. Sunlight filters through the glass and creates breathtaking effects. The shadows cast in some churches can be particularly lovely.

Stalactites: line formations that hang from the ceilings of caves (stalagmites on the other hand, point up from the ground).

Stucco: ornamental reliefs made of plaster, marble dust, sand or other materials – used to cover or decorate architectural projects, cornices, or sculptural models.

Suit of armor: this word defines the whole get-up of metal and leather "clothes" used by soldiers in battle – once upon a time: helmets, arm guards, breastplates, shields, etc.

Tabernacle: a niche, or small chapel where sacred images are

Tambour: drum used as the base for a dome, shaped like a cylinder or another geometrical form

Tapestry: a decorative textile woven on a loom by artisans or artists – with wool, silk, and other threads and materials – used to reproduce a design drawn on pasteboards first. Tapestries were meant to be hung on walls.

Telescope: very powerful scientific instrument used by astronomers to observe heavenly bodies

Tepidarium: the warm room between the cold *frigidarium* and the hot *calidarium* in ancient Roman baths. In gardens, it is a covered cast-iron and glass structure used for protecting plants during the Winter.

Terracotta: a type of ceramic that is molded, dried, and then baked at a high temperature – commonly used for pots, dishes, and especially the bricks for buildings, sidewalks, and roofs.

Tile: square of wood, marble, terracotta, ceramic, bronze or other materials used to decorate doors, ceilings or cornices.

Tombstones: a marble or stone slab used to cover a tomb – often found on the floors of churches.

Triphora: window divided into three identical openings by columns or set in stone.

Vault: covering formed by variously shaped – dates to antiquity

who are these people?

Brief description of people mentioned in this guide

Acuto, Giovanni (John Hawkwood, known as *Giovanni Acuto*, 1320-1394), British mercenary leader.
Alberti, important Florentine family.
Alberti, Leon Battista (1406-1472), architect, writer, and poet.
Albizi, important Florentine family.
Alfieri, Vittorio (1749-1803), poet and tragedy writer.
Alighieri, Dante (1265-1321), poet, wrote the *Divine Comedy*. He was exiled in 1302 for his political alliance with the White Guelphs.
Ambrogio (330 circa-397), Bishop and patron saint of Milan.
Amidei, important Florentine family.
Ammannati, Bartolomeo (1511-1592), sculptor and architect.
Andrea del Castagno (1419-1457), painter.
Andrea di Bonaiuto (1343-1377), painter.
Andrea Pisano (1290-1349), sculptor and architect.
Antonino (1389-1549), saint, Dominican monk and Bishop of Florence.
Arnoldi, Alberto, 14th-century sculptor and architect.
Arnolfo di Cambio (1245-1302), architect and sculptor.
Atto, Bishop of Florence, circa 1000 AD.

Baccio d'Agnolo (1462-1543), architect and wood-carver.
Baccio da Montelupo (1469-1535), sculptor and architect.
Baglioni, Malatesta (1491-1531), led the Florentine army during the siege by Charles V.
Bardi, important Florentine family.
Bartolini Salimbeni, important Florentine family.
Beato Angelico *see* Fra Angelico.
Beatrice, *see* Portinari, Beatrice.
Béjart, Maurice (born in 1927), French dancer and choreographer.
Benedetto da Maiano (1442-1497), sculptor and architect.
Benedetto da Norcia (480-547), saint, founder of the Benedectine Order.
Berio, Luciano (born in 1925), musician, among the first to focus on electronic music.
Bonaparte, Napoleon (1769-1821), general, French Emperor (when he assumed the title of Napoleon I).
Botticelli, Sandro (1445-1510), painter.

Brancacci, important Florentine family.
Brunelleschi, Filippo (1377-1446), architect.
Buonarroti, Michelangelo (1475-1564), sculptor, painter, architect, and poet who lived in Florence and Rome.
Buondelmonti, Buondelmonte dei, young Florentine who was killed after refusing to marry a daughter of Amidei family. His death in 1215 triggered the battle between the Guelphs and the Ghibellines.
Buontalenti, Bernardo (known as *Bernardo of the Pinwheels*, 1536-1608), architect and set designer, also the impresario of Medici parties.
Burton, Richard (1925-1984), theater and film actor from England.

Cappello, Bianca (1543-1587), second wife of Francesco I dei Medici.
Capponi, important Florentine family.
Capponi, Piero (1446-1496), Florentine politician who opposed Charles VIII of France and was able to work out an autonomy pact for Florence after the French invasion.
Caravaggio (Michelangelo Merisi, known as *Caravaggio*, 1571-1610), painter.
Cecilia, 3rd-century saint and Christian martyr.
Cellini, Benvenuto (1500-1571), sculptor, goldsmith, and writer.
Charlemagne (742-814), French king who conquered Italy after defeating the Lombards. Pope Leo III crowned him Holy Roman Emperor.
Charles V (1500-1558), emperor of the Holy Roman Empire.
Charles VIII (1470-1498), French king who invaded Italy and occupied Florence, Rome, and Naples. He was later defeated at Fornovo.
Cherubini, Luigi (1760-1842), musician.
Cimabue (Cenni di Pepo, known as *Cimabue*), 13th-century painter.
Ciriffo, 16th-century pirate.
Cosma e Damiano, brothers, both saints and Christian martyrs, who lived in the 3rd-century AD, patron saints of physicians.
Cuttraputti Rajaram, Indian prince who died in Florence in 1870, buried at the Cascine park.

Dante, *see* Alighieri, Dante.
Danti, Egnazio (1536-1586), mathematician and astronomer.
Davanzati, important Florentine family.
Davizzi, important Florentine family.
Decio (200-251), Roman emperor.
De Fabris, Emilio (1808-1883), architect.
Della Robbia, family of sculptors and ceramics artisans, who left a number of their works in Florence and throughout Tuscany: Luca (1400-1482), Andrea (1435-1528), and Giovanni (1469-1529).
Demidoff, Paolo (1829-1885), prince born in Russia.
Desiderio da Settignano (1430-1464), sculptor.

Domenico di Guzmán (1170-1221), saint, founder of the Dominican Order.

Donatello (Donato di Niccolò di Betto Bardi, known as *Donatello*, 1386-1466), sculptor.

Donati, Gemma (died in 1340), Dante's wife.

Eleonora di Toledo, *see* Medici, Eleonora dei.

Eligio, saint, Bishop of Rouen, France, in the 7th-century AD.

Eugenio IV (Gabriel Gondulmer, 1383-1447), Pope.

Fattori, Giovanni (1825-1908), Painter in the "Macchiaiolo" movement.

Ferragamo, Salvatore (1898-1960), famous shoe designer.

Filippo, 1st-century saint, and one of the 12 Apostles.

Foscolo, Ugo (1778-1827), poet and writer.

Foraboschi, important Florentine family.

Fra Angelico (Giovanni da Fiesole, known as *Beato Angelico* or *Fra Angelico*, 1387-1455), painter.

Fra Bartolomeo (Bartolomeo della Porta, known as *Fra Bartolomeo*, 1472-1517), painter.

Francesco (1181-1226), saint, founder of Franciscan Order.

Gaddi, Agnolo (died in 1396), painter, son of Taddeo.

Gaddi, Taddeo (1290-1366), painter.

Galilei, Galileo (1564-1642), physicist, mathematician, astronomer, philosopher.

Garibaldi, Giuseppe (1807-1882), general who led "dei Mille" movement, a major figure in Italy's reunification ("Risorgimento").

Ghiberti, Lorenzo (1378-1455), sculptor, goldsmith, architect.

Ghirlandaio, Domenico (Domenico Bigordi, known as *Ghirlandaio*, 1449-1494), painter.

Giambologna (Jean Boulogne, known as *Giambologna*, 1529-1608), sculptor and architect.

Giotto di Bondone (1267-1337, known as *Giotto*), painter and architect.

Giovanni Battista, patron saint of Florence.

Giovanni dalle Bande Nere, *see* Medici, Giovanni dei.

Giovanni Gualberto (995-1073), saint and founder of the Vallombrosian Order – involved in battling Bishops.

Giovanni the 23rd (Baldassarre Cossa, 1370-1419), antipope.

Giuliano da Maiano (1432-1490), architect and sculptor.

Gozzoli, Benozzo (1420-1497), painter.

Habakkuk, prophet of the Old Testament, lived in 7th-century BC.

Ildebrando, Bishop who lived around 1000 AD.

Jacopo di Lusitania, Archibishop of Lisbon in 15th-century.
Jacopo il Bavaro, Bishop of Fiesole who lived around 1000 AD.
Jeremiah, Old Testament prophet from 7th-century BC.
John the Evangelist, saint, one of the 12 Apostles, wrote a Gospel and lived in the 1st-century AD.

Lega, Silvestro (1826-1895), painter in the "Macchiaiolo" movement.
Leonardo da Vinci (1452-1519), artist and scientist.
Lippi, Filippino (1457-1504, known as *Fra Lippi*), painter.
Lorena, Ferdinando III di (1769-1824), Grand Duke of Tuscany.
Lorena, Francesco di (1708-1765), Duke of Lorena, Grand Duke of Tuscany – and from 1745, the Emperor of Austria – known as Francesco I.
Lorena, Leopoldo II di (known as *Canapone*, 1797-1870), last Grand Duke of Tuscany.
Lorena, Pietro Leopoldo di (1747-1792), Grand Duke of Tuscany.
Lorenzo, 3rd-century saint and Christian martyr.
Lorenzo Monaco (Pietro di Giovanni, known as *Lorenzo Monaco*, 1370-1423), Sienese painter.
Luke the Evangelist, saint, writer of a Gospel, lived in the 1st-century AD.

Machiavelli, Niccolò (1469-1527), Florentine writer and politician.
Malatesta, Sigismondo Pandolfo, Lord of Rimini in 15th-century.
Manetti, Giuseppe, 18th-century architect.
Manfredi, Astorre, Lord of Faenza in 15th-century.
Mark the Evangelist, saint, writer of a Gospel, lived in the 1st-century AD.
Mario, Caio (156-86 BC), Roman politician, led Democratic faction against Silla.
Mariotti, Mario (1936-1997), Florentine artist.
Martini, Simone (1284-1344), Sienese painter.
Masaccio (Tommaso di Ser Giovanni, known as *Masaccio*, 1401-1428), painter.
Maso di Banco, 14th-century painter.
Masolino da Panicale (Tommaso di Cristoforo Fini, known as *Masolino da Panicale*, 1383-1447), painter.
Medici, important Florentine family.
Medici, Alessandro dei (1512-1537), first Duke of Florence.
Medici, Anna Maria Luisa dei (1667-1743), daughter of Cosimo III and sister of Gian Gastone.
Medici, Bia dei (Maria known as *Bia*, 1540-1557), First-born child of Cosimo I.

Medici, Bianca dei, Lorenzo the Magnificent's sister.
Medici, Cosimo I dei (1519-1574), first Grand Duke of Tuscany.
Medici, Cosimo II dei (1590-1621), Grand Duke of Tuscany.
Medici, Cosimo the Elder (1389-1464), banker, politician, and first Lord of Florence.
Medici, Eleonora (Eleonora di Toledo, 1522-1562), wife of Cosimo I.
Medici, Ferdinando I dei (1549-1609), Grand Duke of Tuscany.
Medici, Ferdinando II dei (1610-1670), Grand Duke of Tuscany.
Medici, Francesco I dei (1541-1587), Grand Duke of Tuscany.
Medici, Gian Gastone dei (1671-1737), last Grand Duke in the Medici family.
Medici, Giovanni dei (known as *Giovanni dalle Bande Nere*, 1498-1526), leader of mercenaries, son of Giovanni dei Medici and Caterina Sforza, father of Cosimo dei Medici – the first Grand Duke.
Medici, Giovanni dei (1543-1562), Fourth-born child of Cosimo I.
Medici, Giovanni di Bicci (1360-1429), father of Cosimo the Elder.
Medici, Giuliano dei (1453-1478), Lorenzo the Magnificent's brother; victim of the Pazzi Conspiracy.
Medici, Giuliano dei, Duke of Nemours (1478-1516), Lorenzo the Magnificent's son.
Medici, Lorenzo dei (known as *Lorenzo the Magnificent*, 1449-1492), Lord of Florence, writer and patron of arts.
Medici, Lorenzo II dei, Duke of Urbino (1492-1519), grandson of Lorenzo the Magnificent.
Medici, Maria dei, sister of Lorenzo the Magnificent.
Medici, Nannina dei, sister of Lorenzo the Magnificent.
Medici, Piero dei (known as *Piero "the Gouty,"* 1416-1469), Lord of Florence before his son Lorenzo.
Medici, Piero dei (1472-1503), Lorenzo the Magnificent's son.
Michelangelo, *see* Buonarroti, Michelangelo.
Michelozzo (Michelozzo di Bartolomeo, 1396-1473), architect and sculptor.
Michelucci, Giovanni (1821-1990), architect and urban planner.
Miniato, 3rd-century saint and martyr.
Mino da Fiesole (1429-1484), sculptor.

Nanni di Banco (Giovanni di Antonio di Banco, known as *Nanni di Banco*, 1373-1421), sculptor.
Napoleon, *see* Bonaparte, Napoleon.
Niccolò da Tolentino, 15th-century knight.
Noah, Biblical patriarch.
Novelli, Antonio, 16th-century sculptor, student of Giambologna.

Orcagna (Andrea di Cione, known as *l'Orcagna*), 16th-century sculptor, painter, and architect.

Ordelaffi, Cecco, Lord of Forlì in the 15th-century.

Paolo (Saulo, 5 BC-67 AD), saint.
Paolo Uccello (Paolo di Dono, known as *Paolo Uccello,* 1397-1475), painter.
Parigi, Alfonso (1606-1656), architect, son of Giulio Parigi.
Parigi, Giulio (1571-1635), architect, etcher, set designer.
Paulovna, Anna, daughter of Czar Pavel I of Russia.
Pavel I Petrovič (1757-1801), Czar of Russia.
Pazzi, important Florentine family.
Pazzi, Pazzino dei, 11th-century Florentine knight in the First Crusade .
Pericoli, Niccolò (known as *il Tribolo*, 1500-1558), sculptor, architect, and engineer.
Peruzzi, important Florentine family.
Petrarca, Francesco (1304-1374), poet.
Pietro (Simone bar-Jona), 1st-century saint. The first of the 12 Apostles.
Pietro da Verona (1203-1252), saint and martyr.
Pietro Igneo, Vallombrosian monk from 11th-century.
Pietro Leopoldo, *see* Lorena, Pietro Leopoldo di.
Pietro Mezzabarba, 11th-century Bishop of Florence.
Pio II (Enea Silvio Piccolomini, 1405-1464), Pope.
Pio V (Antonio Michele Ghislieri, 1504-1572), Pope.
Pitti, important Florentine family.
Pitti, Luca (1394-1472), banker, commissioned Pitti Palace construction.
Poggi, Giuseppe (1811-1901), architect and urban planner.
Portinari Beatrice, young Florentine loved by Dante Alighieri – the inspiration for his work.

Raphael, *see* Sanzio,Raphael.
Riccardi, Gabriello, 17th-century Florentine noble.
Ristoro, 13th-century monk and architect.
Romolo, Patron Saint of Fiesole.
Rossini, Gioachino (1792-1868), musician.
Roster, Giacomo, 19th-century architect and horticulture enthusiast.

Sangallo, Antonio da (1483-1546), architect, Giuliano's grandson.
Sanzio, Raphael (1483-1520), painter born in Urbino.
Sassetti, important Florentine family.
Savoia, (also known as the *House of Savoy),* Italian royal family who ruled from the reunification of Italy through 1946.
Savonarola, Girolamo (1452-1498), Dominican monk and prior of the S. Marco monastery in Florence. He fought to bring a higher morality to

both politics and the Church. However, after crossing Pope Alessandro (Alexander) VI, he was accused of heresy and burned at the stake.

Segaloni, Matteo, 17th-century architect.

Sforza, Galeazzo Maria (1444-1476), Duke of Milan.

Signorini, Telemaco (1835-1901), painter in the "Macchiaiolo" movement.

Silla, Lucio Cornelio (138-78 BC), Roman politician, led aristocratic faction against Marius.

Sisto, 13th-century monk and architect.

Spinello Aretino (1350-1410), painter.

Spini, important Florentine family.

Stibbert, Federico, 19th-century British collector and founder of the Stibbert Museum.

Strozzi, important Florentine family.

Strozzi, Filippo, 15th-century Florentine banker.

Sustermans, Giusto (1597-1681), Medici court painter from Flanders.

Talenti, Francesco (1300 ca.-1369), architect and sculptor.

Talenti, Jacopo, 13th-century monk and architect.

Titian, *see* Vecellio, Titian.

Tommaso d'Aquino (1225-1274), philosopher, theologian, and saint.

Totila, 6th-century King of the Ostrogoths who fough the Byzantines in Italy during the Greco-Gothic War

Tribolo, *see* Pericoli, Niccolò.

Uberti, important Florentine family.

Ugo di Toscana (953 around-1001), Marquis of Tuscany.

Uguccioni, important Florentine family.

Vasari, Giorgio (1511-1574), writer, architect, and painter.

Vecellio, Titian (1490-1576), Venetian painter.

Verrocchio (Andrea di Francesco di Cione, known as *il Verrocchio*, 1435-1488), painter, goldsmith, and sculptor.

Versace, Gianni (1946-1997), stylist and costume-designer.

Vittorio Emanuele II di Savoia (1820-1878), first King of Italy.

Willa, Ugo di Toscana's mother, lived in 10th-century.

Zeffirelli, Franco (born in 1923), film director.

Zuccari, Federico (1543-1609), painter and architect.

Printed in Italy
by Nidiaci Grafiche